Barry L

VIN

Barry Lopez was born in   . Chester, New York, in
1945. He grew up in the San Fernando Valley in southern
California and returned in 1956 to New York City, where
he attended high school. Lopez graduated from the University of Notre Dame in 1966, the year his first short stories were published. In 1968, he moved to rural western
Oregon, where he still resides.

Lopez's early essays, articles, book reviews, and fiction
were published in dozens of popular and literary magazines
in the sixties and seventies. Between 1969 and 1971, he
also worked as a stringer for both *The New York Times* and
The Washington Post. In 1976 his first collection of short
fiction, *Desert Notes,* was published, followed in 1978 by his
first major work of nonfiction, *Of Wolves and Men,* a final-
ist for the National Book Award. A collection of short stories, *Winter Count,* received the Distinguished Recognition
Award from Friends of American Writers in 1981, the
same year Lopez became a contributing editor of *Harper's*
magazine, where his essays began to appear regularly.

During the late seventies and early eighties, Lopez traveled extensively throughout northern Alaska and northern
Canada, studying the history and wildlife of the region
with scientists and Yup'ik, Inupiat, and Inuit Eskimo. His
field studies culminated in the landmark book *Arctic Dreams,*
which received the National Book Award in 1986, as well
as other honors.

Lopez's first essay collection, *Crossing Open Ground,* was published in 1988. A second, *About This Life,* incorporating his first memoirs, appeared in 1998. In the nineties, Lopez returned to writing short stories and authored two award-winning collections, *Field Notes* in 1994 and *Light Action in the Caribbean* in 2000.

In 2002 Lopez was elected a Fellow of The Explorers Club. He is a recipient of the Award in Literature from the American Academy of Arts and Letters, the John Hay and John Burroughs medals, and fellowships from the Guggenheim, Lannan, and National Science foundations. In 2003 he was named the first Distinguished University Scholar at Texas Tech University where, together with Edward O. Wilson, he designed an undergraduate degree program that combines study in the sciences and humanities.

VINTAGE LOPEZ

Barry Lopez

VINTAGE BOOKS

A Division of Random House, Inc.

New York

CONTENTS

VINTAGE **LOPEZ**

LANDSCAPE AND NARRATIVE

One summer evening in a remote village in the Brooks Range of Alaska, I sat among a group of men listening to hunting stories about the trapping and pursuit of animals. I was particularly interested in several incidents involving wolverine, in part because a friend of mine was studying wolverine in Canada, among the Cree, but, too, because I find this animal such an intense creature. To hear about its life is to learn more about fierceness.

Wolverine are not intentionally secretive, hiding their lives from view, but they are seldom observed. The range of their known behavior is less than that of, say, bears or wolves. Still, that evening no gratuitous details were set out. This was somewhat odd, for wolverine easily excite the imagination; they can loom suddenly in the landscape with authority, with an aura larger than their compact physical dimensions, drawing one's immediate and complete attention. Wolverine also have a deserved reputation for resoluteness in the worst winters, for ferocious strength.

But neither did these attributes induce the men to embellish.

I listened carefully to these stories, taking pleasure in the sharply observed detail surrounding the dramatic thread of events. The story I remember most vividly was about a man hunting a wolverine from a snow machine in the spring. He followed the animal's tracks for several miles over rolling tundra in a certain valley. Soon he caught sight ahead of a dark spot on the crest of a hill—the wolverine pausing to look back. The hunter was catching up, but each time he came over a rise the wolverine was looking back from the next rise, just out of range. The hunter topped one more rise and met the wolverine bounding toward him. Before he could pull his rifle from its scabbard the wolverine flew across the engine cowl and the windshield, hitting him square in the chest. The hunter scrambled his arms wildly, trying to get the wolverine out of his lap, and fell over as he did so. The wolverine jumped clear as the snow machine rolled over, and fixed the man with a stare. He had not bitten, not even scratched the man. Then the wolverine walked away. The man thought of reaching for the gun, but no, he did not.

The other stories were like this, not so much making a point as evoking something about contact with wild animals that would never be completely understood.

When the stories were over, four or five of us walked out of the home of our host. The surrounding land, in the persistent light of a far northern summer, was still visible for miles—the striated, pitched massifs of the Brooks Range; the shy, willow-lined banks of the John River flowing south from Anaktuvuk Pass; and the flat tundra plain, opening with great affirmation to the north. The landscape seemed alive because of the stories. It was precisely these ocherous tones, this kind of willow, exactly this austerity that had informed the wolverine narratives. I felt exhilaration, and a deeper confirmation of the stories. The mundane tasks which awaited me I anticipated now with pleasure. The stories had renewed in me a sense of the purpose of my life.

This feeling, an inexplicable renewal of enthusiasm after storytelling, is familiar to many people. It does not seem to matter greatly what the subject is, as long as the context is intimate and the story is told for its own sake, not forced to serve merely as the vehicle for an idea. The tone of the story need not be solemn. The darker aspects of life need not be ignored. But I think intimacy is indispensable—a feeling that derives from the listener's trust and a storyteller's certain knowledge of his subject and regard for his audience. This intimacy deepens if the storyteller tempers his authority with humility, or when terms of idiomatic expression, or at least the physical setting for the story, are shared.

I think of two landscapes—one outside the self, the other within. The external landscape is the one we see—not only the line and color of the land and its shading at different times of the day, but also its plants and animals in season, its weather, its geology, the record of its climate and evolution. If you walk up, say, a dry arroyo in the Sonoran Desert you will feel a mounding and rolling of sand and silt beneath your foot that is distinctive. You will anticipate the crumbling of the sedimentary earth in the arroyo bank as your hand reaches out, and in that tangible evidence you will sense a history of water in the region. Perhaps a black-throated sparrow lands in a paloverde bush—the resiliency of the twig under the bird, that precise shade of yellowish-green against the milk-blue sky, the fluttering whir of the arriving sparrow, are what I mean by "the landscape." Draw on the smell of creosote bush, or clack stones together in the dry air. Feel how light is the desiccated dropping of the kangaroo rat. Study an animal track obscured by the wind. These are all elements of the land, and what makes the landscape comprehensible are the relationships between them. One learns a landscape finally not by knowing the name or identity of everything in it, but by perceiving the relationships in it—like that between the sparrow and the twig. The difference between the relationships and the elements is the same as that between written history and a catalog of events.

The second landscape I think of is an interior one, a kind of projection within a person of a part of the exterior landscape. Relationships in the exterior landscape include those that are named and discernible, such as the nitrogen cycle, or a vertical sequence of Ordovician limestone, and others that are uncodified or ineffable, such as winter light falling on a particular kind of granite, or the effect of humidity on the frequency of a blackpoll warbler's burst of song. That these relationships have purpose and order, however inscrutable they may seem to us, is a tenet of evolution. Similarly, the speculations, intuitions, and formal ideas we refer to as "mind" are a set of relationships in the interior landscape with purpose and order; some of these are obvious, many impenetrably subtle. The shape and character of these relationships in a person's thinking, I believe, are deeply influenced by where on this earth one goes, what one touches, the patterns one observes in nature—the intricate history of one's life in the land, even a life in the city, where wind, the chirp of birds, the line of a falling leaf, are known. These thoughts are arranged, further, according to the thread of one's moral, intellectual, and spiritual development. The interior landscape responds to the character and subtlety of an exterior landscape; the shape of the individual mind is affected by land as it is by genes.

In stories like those I heard at Anaktuvuk Pass about wolverine, the relationship between separate elements in the land is set forth clearly. It is put in a simple framework of sequential incidents and apposite detail. If the exterior landscape is limned well, the listener often feels that he has heard something pleasing and authentic—trustworthy. We derive this sense of confidence I think not so much from verifiable truth as from an understanding that lying has played no role in the narrative. The storyteller is obligated to engage the reader with a precise vocabulary, to set forth a coherent and dramatic rendering of incidents—and to be ingenuous.

When one hears a story one takes pleasure in it for different reasons—for the euphony of its phrases, an aspect of the plot, or because one identifies with one of the characters. With certain stories certain individuals may experience a deeper, more profound sense of well-being. This latter phenomenon, in my understanding, rests at the heart of storytelling as an elevated experience among aboriginal peoples. It results from bringing two landscapes together. The exterior landscape is organized according to principles or laws or tendencies beyond human control. It is understood to contain an integrity that is beyond human analysis and unimpeachable. Insofar as the storyteller depicts various subtle and obvious relationships in the exterior landscape accurately in his story, and insofar as he orders them along traditional lines of meaning to create the narrative, the narrative will "ring true." The listener who "takes the story to heart" will feel a pervasive sense of congruence within himself and also with the world.

Among the Navajo and, as far as I know, many other native peoples, the land is thought to exhibit a sacred order. That order is the basis of ritual. The rituals themselves reveal the power in that order. Art, architecture, vocabulary, and costume, as well as ritual, are derived from the perceived natural order of the universe—from observations and meditations on the exterior landscape. An indigenous philosophy—metaphysics, ethics, epistemology, aesthetics, and logic—may also be derived from a people's continuous attentiveness to both the obvious (scientific) and ineffable (artistic) orders of the local landscape. Each individual, further, undertakes to order his interior landscape according to the exterior landscape. To succeed in this means to achieve a balanced state of mental health.

I think of the Navajo for a specific reason. Among the various sung ceremonies of this people—Enemyway, Coyoteway, Red Antway, Uglyway—is one called Beautyway. In the Navajo view, the elements of one's interior life— one's psychological makeup and moral bearing—are subject to a persistent principle of disarray. Beautyway is, in part, a spiritual invocation of the order of the exterior universe, that irreducible, holy complexity that manifests itself as all things changing through time (a Navajo definition of beauty, hózhǫ́ǫ́). The purpose of this invocation is to recreate in the individual who is the subject of the Beautyway ceremony that same order, to make the individual again a reflection of the myriad enduring relationships of the landscape.

I believe story functions in a similar way. A story draws on relationships in the exterior landscape and projects them onto the interior landscape. The purpose of storytelling is to achieve harmony between the two landscapes, to use all the elements of story—syntax, mood, figures of speech—in a harmonious way to reproduce the harmony of the land in the individual's interior. Inherent in story is the power to reorder a state of psychological confusion through contact with the pervasive truth of those relationships we call "the land."

These thoughts, of course, are susceptible to interpretation. I am convinced, however, that these observations can be applied to the kind of prose we call nonfiction as well as to traditional narrative forms such as the novel and the short story, and to some poems. Distinctions between fiction and nonfiction are sometimes obscured by arguments over what constitutes "the truth." In the aboriginal literature I am familiar with, the first distinction made among narratives is to separate the authentic from the inauthentic. Myth, which we tend to regard as fictitious or "merely metaphorical," is as authentic, as real, as the story of a wolverine in a man's lap. (A distinction is made, of course, about the elevated nature of myth—and frequently the circumstances of myth-telling are more rigorously prescribed than those for the telling of legends or vernacular stories—but all of these narratives are rooted in the local landscape. To violate *that* connection is to call the narrative itself into question.)

The power of narrative to nurture and heal, to repair a spirit in disarray, rests on two things: the skillful invocation of unimpeachable sources and a listener's knowledge that no hypocrisy or subterfuge is involved. This last simple fact is to me one of the most imposing aspects of the Holocene history of man.

We are more accustomed now to thinking of "the truth" as something that can be explicitly stated, rather than as something that can be evoked in a metaphorical way outside science and Occidental culture. Neither can truth be reduced to aphorism or formulas. It is something alive and unpronounceable. Story creates an atmosphere in which it becomes discernible as a pattern. For a storyteller to insist on relationships that do not exist is to lie. Lying is the opposite of story. (I do not mean to confuse ignorance with deception, or to imply that a storyteller can perceive all that is inherent in the land. Every storyteller falls short of a perfect limning of the landscape—perception and language both fail. But to make up something that is not there, something which can never be corroborated in the land, to knowingly set forth a false relationship, is to be lying, no longer telling a story.)

Because of the intricate, complex nature of the land, it is not always possible for a storyteller to grasp what is contained in a story. The intent of the storyteller, then, must be to evoke, honestly, some single aspect of all that the land contains. The storyteller knows that because different individuals grasp the story at different levels, the focus of his regard for truth must be at the primary one—with who was there, what happened, when, where, and why things occurred. The story will then possess similar truth at other levels—the integrity inherent at the primary level of meaning will be conveyed everywhere else. As long as the storyteller carefully describes the order before him, and uses his storytelling skill to heighten and emphasize certain relationships, it is even possible for the story to be more successful than the storyteller himself is able to imagine.

I would like to make a final point about the wolverine stories I heard at Anaktuvuk Pass. I wrote down the details afterward, concentrating especially on aspects of the biology and ecology of the animals. I sent the information on to my friend living with the Cree. When, many months later, I saw him, I asked whether the Cree had enjoyed these insights of the Nunamiut into the nature of the wolverine. What had they said?

"You know," he told me, "how they are. They said, 'That could happen.'"

In these uncomplicated words the Cree declared their own knowledge of the wolverine. They acknowledged that although they themselves had never seen the things the Nunamiut spoke of, they accepted them as accurate observations, because they did not consider story a context for misrepresentation. They also preserved their own dignity by not overstating their confidence in the Nunamiut, a distant and unknown people.

Whenever I think of this courtesy on the part of the Cree I think of the dignity that is ours when we cease to demand the truth and realize that the best we can have of those substantial truths that guide our lives is metaphorical—a story. And the most of it we are likely to discern comes only when we accord one another the respect the Cree showed the Nunamiut. Beyond this—that the interior landscape is a metaphorical representation of the exterior landscape, that the truth reveals itself most fully not in dogma but in the paradox, irony, and contradictions that distinguish compelling narratives—beyond this there are only failures of imagination: reductionism in science; fundamentalism in religion; fascism in politics.

Our national literatures should be important to us insofar as they sustain us with illumination and heal us. They can always do that so long as they are written with respect for both the source and the reader, and with an understanding of why the human heart and the land have been brought together so regularly in human history.

LEARNING TO SEE

In June 1989, I received a puzzling letter from the Amon Carter Museum in Fort Worth, Texas, an invitation to speak at the opening of a retrospective of the work of Robert Adams. The show, "To Make It Home: Photographs of the American West, 1965–1985," had been organized by the Philadelphia Museum of Art and would travel to the Los Angeles County Museum and the Corcoran Gallery of Art in Washington, D.C., before being installed at the Amon Carter, an institution renowned for its photographic collections, in the spring of 1990.

Robert Adams, an un-self-promoting man who has published no commercially prominent book of photographs, is routinely referred to as one of the most important landscape photographers in America, by both art critics and his colleagues. His black-and-white images are intelligently composed and morally engaged. They're also hopeful, despite their sometimes depressing subject matter—brutalized landscapes and the venality of the American Dream as revealed in suburban life. Adams doesn't hold himself apart from what he indicts. He photographs with compassion and he doesn't scold. His pictures are also accessible, to such a degree that many of them seem casual. In 1981 he published *Beauty in Photography: Essays in Defense of Traditional Values,* one of the clearest statements of artistic responsibility ever written by a photographer.

If there is such a thing as an ideal of stance, technique, vision, and social contribution toward which young photographers might aspire, it's embodied in this man.

I suspected the Amon Carter had inadvertently invited the wrong person to speak. I'd no knowledge of the history of American photography sufficient to situate Robert Adams in it. I couldn't speak to the technical perfection of his prints. I'd no credentials as an art critic. As an admirer of the work, of course, I'd have something to say, but it could only be that, the words of an amateur who admired Adams's accomplishment.

I wondered for days what prompted the invitation. For about fifteen years, before putting my cameras down on September 13, 1981, never to pick them up again, I'd worked as a landscape photographer, but it was unlikely anyone at the Amon Carter knew this. I'd visited the museum in the fall of 1986 to see some of their luminist paintings and had met several of the curators, but our conversations could not have left anyone with the impression that I had the background to speak about Adams's work.

I finally decided to say yes. I wrote and told the person coordinating the program, Mary Lampe, that though I didn't feel qualified to speak I admired Mr. Adams's work, and further, I presumed an affinity with his pursuits and ideals as set forth in *Beauty in Photography*. And I told her I intended to go back and study the work of Paul Strand, Wynn Bullock, Minor White, Harry Callahan, and others who'd been an influence on my own work and thought, in order to prepare my lecture.

Months later, when I arrived at the museum, I asked Ms. Lampe how they had come to invite me and not someone more qualified. She said Mr. Adams had asked them to do so. I sensed she believed Robert Adams and I were good friends and I had to tell her I didn't know him at all. We'd never met, never corresponded, had not spoken on the phone. I was unaware, even, that it was "Bob" Adams, as Ms. Lampe called him.

"But why did you agree to come?" she asked.

"Out of respect for the work," I said. "Out of enthusiasm for the work." I also explained that I was intimidated by the prospect, and that sometimes I felt it was good to act on things like that.

Ms. Lampe subsequently sent Robert Adams a tape of my talk. He and I later met and we now correspond and speak on the phone regularly. He set the course of our friendship in the first sentence of a letter he wrote me after hearing my presentation. "Your willingness to speak in my behalf," he wrote, "confirms my belief in the community of artists."

He believed from work of mine that he'd read that we shared a sensibility, that we asked similar questions about the relationship between culture and landscape, and that our ethical leanings and our sense of an artist's social responsibility were similar. He later told me that for these reasons he'd given my name, hopefully but somewhat face-tiously, to Ms. Lampe, not knowing the curators and I were acquainted and that they would write me.

I've long been attracted to the way visual artists like Robert Adams imagine the world. The emotional impact of their composition of space and light is as clarifying for me as immersion in a beautifully made story. As with the work of a small group of poets I read regularly—Robert Hass, Pattiann Rogers, Garrett Hongo—I find healing in their expressions. I find reasons not to give up.

Though I no longer photograph, I have maintained since 1981 a connection with photographers and I keep up a sort of running conversation with several of them. We talk about the fate of photography in the United States, where of course art is increasingly more commodified and where, with the advent of computer manipulation, photography is the art most likely to mislead. Its history as a purveyor of objective reality, the idea that "the camera never lies," is specious, certainly; but with some artistic endeavors, say those of Cartier-Bresson, Aaron Siskind, or W. Eugene Smith, and in the fields of documentary photography, which would include some news photography, and nature photography, one can assert that the authority of the image lies with the subject. With the modern emphasis on the genius of the individual artist, however, and with the arrival of computer imaging, authority in these areas now more often lies with the photographer. This has become true to such an extent that the reversal that's occurred—the photographer, not the subject, is in charge—has caused the rules of evidence to be changed in courts of law; and it has foisted upon an unwitting public a steady stream, for example, of fabricated images of wildlife.

As a beginning photographer I was most attracted to color and form, to the emotional consequence of line. It is no wonder, looking back now, that I pored over the images of someone like Edward Weston, or that I felt isolated in some of my pursuits because at the time few serious photographers outside Ernst Haas and Eliot Porter worked as I did in color. I wanted to photograph the streaming of light. For a long while it made no difference whether that light was falling down the stone walls of a building in New York or lambent on the corrugations of a wheat field. Ansel Adams was suggested to me early on as a model, but he seemed to my eye inclined to overstate. I wanted the sort of subtlety I would later come to admire in Bob Adams's work and in the aerial photographs of Emmet Gowin.

The more I gravitated as a writer toward landscape as a context in which to work out what I was thinking as a young man about issues like justice, tolerance, ambiguity, and compassion, the more I came to concentrate on landforms as a photographer. I valued in particular the work of one or two wildlife photographers shooting *in situ,* in the bush. (I remember enthusiastically contacting friends about John Dominis's groundbreaking portfolio of African cat photographs, which appeared in three successive issues of *Life* in January 1967.) But I was not inclined toward mastering the kind of technical skill it took to make such photographs. More fundamentally, I had misgivings about what I regarded as invasions of the privacy of wild animals. The latter notion I thought so personal an idea I kept it mostly to myself; today, of course, it's a central concern of wildlife photographers, especially for a contingent that includes Frans Lanting, the late Michio Hoshino, Gary Braasch, Tui De Roy, and the team of Susan Middleton and David Liittschwager.

I began photographing in a conscientious way in the summer of 1965. I was soon concentrating on landscapes, and in the mid-1970s, with a small list of publication credits behind me, I made an appointment to see Joe Scherschel, an assistant director of the photographic staff at *National Geographic.* He told me frankly that though my landscape portfolio was up to the standards of the magazine, the paucity of wildlife images and human subjects made it unlikely that he could offer me any assignments. In response I remember thinking this was unlikely to change, for either of us. Discouraged, I started to scale back the effort to market my photographs and to make part of my living that way. I continued to make pictures, and I was glad that much of this work was still effectively represented by a stock agency in New York; but by 1978 I knew photography for me was becoming more a conscious exercise in awareness, a technique for paying attention. It would finally turn into a sequestered exploration of light and spatial volume.

Three events in the late 1970s changed the way I understood myself as a photographer. One summer afternoon I left the house for an appointment with an art director in a nearby city. Strapped to the seat of my motorcycle was a box of photographs, perhaps three hundred images representative of the best work I had done. The two-lane road I traveled winds gently through steep mountainous country.

When I got to town the photographs were gone. I never found a trace of them, though I searched every foot of the road for two days. The loss dismantled my enthusiasm for photography so thoroughly that I took it for a message to do something else.

In the summer of 1976 my mother was dying of cancer. To ease her burden, and to brighten the sterile room in Lenox Hill Hospital in New York where she lay dying, I made a set of large Cibachrome prints from some of my 35-mm Kodachrome images—a white horse standing in a field of tall wild grasses bounded by a white post-and-plank fence; a faded pink boat trailer from the 1940s, abandoned in the woods; a small copse of quaking aspen, their leaves turning bright yellow on the far side of a remote mountain swamp. It was the only set of prints I would ever make. As good as they were, the change in color balance and the loss of transparency and contrast when compared with the originals, the reduction in sharpness, created a deep doubt about ever wanting to do such a thing again. I hung the images in a few shows, then put them away. I knew if I didn't start developing and printing my own images, I wouldn't be entering any more shows.

I winced whenever I saw my photographs reproduced in magazines and books, but I made my peace with that. Time-Life Books was publishing a series then called *American Wilderness,* each volume of which was devoted to a different landscape—the Maine woods, the Cascade Mountains, the Grand Canyon. I was pleased to see my work included in these volumes, but I realized that just as the distance between what I saw and what I was able to record was huge, so was that between what I recorded and what people saw.

Seeing the printed images on the page was like finding one's haiku published as nineteen-syllable poems.

The third event occurred around the first serious choice I made as a photographer to concentrate on a limited subject. The subject was always light, but I wanted to explore a single form, which turned out to be the flow of water in creeks and rivers near my home. I photographed in every season, when the water was high in February and March, when it was low in August, when it was transparent in July, when it was an opaque jade in December. In 1980 I began to photograph moving water in moonlight, exposures of twenty-five or thirty minutes. These images suffered from reciprocity failure—the color balance in them collapsed—but they also recorded something extraordinary, a pattern of flow we cannot actually see. They revealed the organizing principle logicians would one day call a strange attractor.

The streaming of water around a rock is one of the most complex motions of which human beings are aware. The change from a laminar, more or less uniform flow to turbulent flow around a single rock is so abstruse a transition mathematically that even the most sophisticated Cray computer cannot make it through to a satisfactory description.

Aesthetically, of course, no such difficulty exists. The eye dotes on the shift, delights in the scintillating sheeting, the roll-off of light around a rock, like hair responding to the stroke of a brush. Sometimes I photographed the flow of water in sunshine at 1/2000 of a second and then later I'd photograph the same rock in moonlight. Putting the photos side by side, I could see something hidden beneath the dazzle of the high-speed image that compared with our renderings of the Milky Way from space: the random pin-dot infernos of our own and every other sun form a spiraling, geometrical shape motionless to our eyes. In the moonlit photographs, the stray streaks from errant water splashes were eliminated (in light that weak, they occur too quickly to be recorded); what was etched on the film instead were orderly, fundamental lines of flow, created by particle after illuminated particle of gleaming water, as if each were a tracer bullet. (Years later, reading *Chaos,* James Gleick's lucid report on chaos theory, I would sit bolt upright in my chair. What I'd photographed was the deep pattern in turbulence, the clothing, as it were, of the strange attractor.)

In the months I worked at making these photographs, I came to realize I actually had two subjects as a photographer. First, these still images of a moving thing, a living thing—as close as I would probably ever come to fully photographing an animal. Second, natural light falling on orchards, images of a subject routinely understood as a still life. The orchards near me were mostly filbert orchards. In their change of color and form through the seasons, in the rain and snow that fell through them, in crows that sat on their winter branches, in leaves accumulated under them on bare dark ground, in the wind that coursed them, in the labyrinths of their limbs, ramulose within the imposed order of the orchard plot, I saw the same profundity of life I found in literature.

This was all work I was eager to do, but I would never get to it.

In September 1981 I was working in the Beaufort Sea off the north coast of Alaska with several marine biologists. We were conducting a food-chain survey intended to provide baseline data to guide offshore oil drilling, an impulsive and politically motivated development program funded by the Bureau of Land Management and pushed hard at the time by the Reagan government. On September 12, three of us rendezvoused at Point Barrow with a National Oceanic and Atmospheric Administration research vessel, the *Oceanographer*. They hoisted us, our gear, and our twenty-foot Boston Whaler aboard and we sailed west into pack ice in the northern Chukchi Sea.

Scientific field research is sometimes a literally bloody business. In our study we were trying to determine the flow of energy through various "levels" (artificially determined) of the marine food web. To gather data we retrieved plankton and caught fish with different sorts of traps and trawls, and we examined the contents of bearded seal, ringed seal, and spotted seal stomachs. To accomplish the latter, we shot and killed the animals. Shooting seals located us squarely in the moral dilemma of our work, and it occasioned talk aboard the *Oceanographer* about the barbarousness of science. The irony here was that without these data creatures like the ringed seal could not be afforded legal protection against oil development. The killings were a manifestation of the perversions in our age, our Kafkaesque predicaments.

I was disturbed by the fatal aspects of our work, as were my companions, but I willingly participated. I would later write an essay about the killing, but something else happened during that trip, less dramatic and more profound in its consequences for me.

Late one afternoon, working our way back to the

Oceanographer through a snow squall, the three of us came upon a polar bear. We decided to follow him for a few minutes and I got out my cameras. The bear, swimming through loose pack ice, was clearly annoyed by our presence, though in our view we were maintaining a reasonable distance. He very soon climbed out on an ice floe, crossed it, and dropped into open water on the far side. We had to go the long way around in the workboat, but we caught up. He hissed at us and otherwise conveyed his irritation, but we continued idling along beside him.

Eventually we backed off. The bear disappeared in gauze curtains of blowing snow. We returned to the *Oceanographer,* to a warm meal and dry clothes.

Once the boat was secure and our scientific samples squared away in the lab, I went to my cabin. I dropped my pack on the floor, stripped off my heavy clothes, showered, and lay down in my bunk. I tried to recall every detail of the encounter with the bear. What had he been doing when we first saw him? Did he change direction then? How had he proceeded? Exactly how did he climb out of the water onto the ice floe? What were the mechanics of it? When he shook off seawater, how was it different from a dog shucking water? When he hissed, what color was the inside of his mouth?

I don't know how long I lay there, a half hour perhaps, but when I was through, when I'd answered these questions and was satisfied that I'd recalled the sequence of events precisely and in sufficient detail, I got up, dressed, and went to dinner. Remembering what happened in an encounter was crucial to my work as a writer, and attending to my cameras during our time with the bear had altered and shrunk my memory of it. While the polar bear was doing something, I was checking f-stops and attempting to frame and focus from a moving boat.

I regarded the meeting as a warning to me as a writer. Having successfully recovered details from each minute, I believed, of that encounter, having disciplined myself to do that, I sensed I wouldn't pick up a camera ever again.

It was not solely contact with this lone bear a hundred miles off the northwest coast of Alaska, of course, that ended my active involvement with photography. The change had been coming for a while. The power of the polar bear's presence, his emergence from the snow squall and his subsequent disappearance, had created an atmosphere in which I could grasp more easily a complex misgiving that had been building in me. I view any encounter with a wild animal in its own territory as a gift, an opportunity to sense the real animal, not the zoo creature, the TV creature, the advertising creature. But this gift had been more overwhelming. In some way the bear had grabbed me by the shirtfront and said, Think about this. Think about what these cameras in your hands are doing.

Years later, I'm still thinking about it. Some of what culminated for me that day is easy to understand. As a writer, I had begun to feel I was missing critical details in situations such as this one because I was distracted. I was also starting to feel uncomfortable about the way photographs tend to collapse events into a single moment, about how much they leave out. (Archeologists face a similar problem when they save only what they recognize from a dig. Years afterward, the context long having been destroyed, the archeologist might wonder what was present that he or she didn't recognize at the time. So begins a reevaluation of the meaning of the entire site.)

I was also disturbed about how nature and landscape photographs, my own and others', were coming to be used, not in advertising where you took your chances (some photographers at that time began labeling their images explicitly: NO TOBACCO, NO ALCOHOL), but in the editorial pages of national magazines. It is a polite fiction of our era that the average person, including the average art director, is more informed about natural history than an educated person was in Columbus's age. Because this is not true, the majority of nature photographers who work out in the field have felt a peculiar burden to record accurately the great range of habitat and animal behavior they see, including nature's "dark" side. (Photographers accepted the fact back then that magazines in the United States, generally speaking, were not interested in photographs of mating animals—unless they were chaste or cute—or in predatory encounters if they were bloody or harrowing, as many were.)

What happened as a result of this convention was that people looking at magazines in the 1970s increasingly came to think of wild animals as vivacious and decorative in the natural world. Promoted as elegant, brave, graceful, sinister, wise, etc., according to their species, animals were deprived of personality and the capacity to be innovative. Every wildlife photographer I know can recount a story of confrontation with an art director in which he or she argued unsuccessfully for an image that told a fuller or a truer story about a particular species of animal in a layout. It was the noble lion, the thieving hyena, and the mischievous monkey, however, who routinely triumphed. A female wolf killing one of her pups, or a male bonobo approaching a female with a prominent erection, was not anything magazine editors were comfortable with.

In the late seventies, I asked around among several publishers to see whether they might have any interest in a series of disturbing photographs made in a zoo by a woman named Ilya. She'd taken them on assignment for *Life,* but very few of them were ever published because she'd concentrated on depicting animals apparently driven insane by their incarceration. I remember as particularly unsettling the look of psychosis in the face of a male lion, its mane twisted into knots. I could develop no interest in publishing her work. An eccentric view, people felt. Too distressing.

So, along with a growing political awareness of endangered landscapes and their indigenous animals in the 1970s came, ironically, a more and more dazzling presentation of those creatures in incomplete and prejudicial ways. Photo editors made them look not like what they were but the way editors wanted them to appear—well-groomed, appropriate to stereotype, and living safely apart from the machinations of human enterprise. To my mind there was little difference then between a *Playboy* calendar and a wildlife calendar. Both celebrated the conventionally gorgeous, the overly endowed, the seductive. I and many other photographers at the time were apprehensive about the implications of this trend.

Another concern I had that September afternoon, a more complicated one, was what was happening to memory in my generation. The advertising injunction to preserve family memories by taking photographs had become so shrill a demand, and the practice had become so compulsive, that recording the event was more important for some than participating in it. The inculcated rationale which grew up around this practice was that to take and preserve family photos was to act in a socially responsible way. The assumption seemed specious to me. My generation was the first to have ready access to inexpensive tape recorders and cameras. Far from recording memories of these talks and events, what we seemed to be doing was storing memories that would never be retrieved, that would never form a coherent narrative. In the same way that our desk drawers and cabinet shelves slowly filled with these "personal" sounds and images, we were beginning, it seemed to me, to live our lives in dissociated bits and pieces. The narrative spine of an individual life was disappearing. The order of events was becoming increasingly meaningless.

This worry, together with the increasingly commercial use to which the work of photographers like myself was being put and the preference for an entertaining but not necessarily coherent landscape of wild animals (images that essentially lied to children), made me more and more reluctant to stay involved. Some of the contemporary photographers I most respect—Lanting, Hoshino, Braasch, De Roy, Jim Brandenburg, Flip Nicklin, Sam Abell, Nick Nichols, Galen Rowell—have managed through the strength of their work and their personal integrity to overcome some of these problems, which are part and parcel of working in a world dominated more and more by commercial interests pursuing business strategies. But I knew I had no gift here to persevere. That realization, and my reluctance to photograph animals in the first place, may have precipitated my decision that day in the Chukchi.

As a writer, I had yet other concerns, peculiar to that discipline. I had begun to wonder whether my searching for the telling photographic image in a situation was beginning to interfere with my writing about what happened. I was someone who took a long time to let a story settle. I'd begun to suspect that the photographs made while I was in a note-taking stage were starting to lock my words into a pattern, and that the pattern was being determined too early. Photographs, in some way, were introducing preconceptions into a process I wanted to keep fluid. I often have no clear idea of what I'm doing. I just act. I pitch in, I try to stay alert to everything around me. I don't want to stop and focus on a finished image, which I'm inclined to do as a photographer. I want, instead, to see a sentence fragment scrawled in my notebook, smeared by rain. I don't want the clean, fixed image right away.

An attentive mind, I'm sure, can see the flaws in my reasoning. Some photographers are doing no more than taking notes when they click the shutter. It's only after a shoot that they discover what the story is. But by trying to both photograph and write, I'd begun to feel I was attempting to create two parallel but independent stories. The effort had become confusing and draining. I let go of photography partly because its defining process, to my mind, was less congruent with the way I wanted to work.

On June 16, 1979, forty-one sperm whales beached themselves at the mouth of the Siuslaw River on the Oregon coast, about one hundred miles from my home. I wrote a long essay about the stranding but didn't start work on it until after I'd spent two days photographing the eclipse of these beasts' lives and the aftermath of their deaths. That was the last time I attempted to do both things.

Perhaps the most rarefied of my concerns about photography that day in the Chukchi was one that lay for me at the heart of photography: recording a fleeting pattern of light in a defined volume of space. Light always attracted me. Indeed, twenty-five years after the fact, I can still vividly recall the light falling at dusk on a windbreak of trees in Mitchell, Oregon. It rendered me speechless when I saw it, and by some magic I managed to get it down on film. The problem of rendering volume in photography, however, was one I never solved beyond employing the conventional solutions of perspective and depth of field. I could recognize spatial volume successfully addressed in the work of other photographers—in Adams's work, for example, partly because so many of his photographs do not have an object as a subject. Finding some way myself to render volume successfully in a photograph would mean, I believed, walking too far away from my work as a writer. And, ultimately, it was as a writer that I felt more comfortable.

I miss making photographs. A short while ago I received a call from a curator at the Whitney Museum in New York named May Castleberry. She had just mounted a show called "Perpetual Mirage: Photographic Narratives of the Desert West" and I had been able to provide some minor assistance with it. She was calling now to pursue a conversation we'd begun at the time about Rockwell Kent, an illustrator, painter, and socialist widely known in the thirties, forties, and fifties. She wanted to hang a selection of his "nocturnes," prints and drawings Kent had made of people under starlit night skies. She was calling to see what I could suggest about his motivation.

Given Kent's leanings toward Nordic myth and legend and his espousal of Teddy Roosevelt's "strenuous life," it seemed obvious to me that he would want to portray his heroic (mostly male) figures against the vault of the heavens. But there were at least two other things at work here, I believed. First, Kent was strongly drawn to high latitudes, like Greenland, where in winter one can view the deep night sky for weeks on end. It was not really the "night" sky, however, he was drawing; it was the sunless sky of a winter day. Quotidian life assumes mythic proportions here not because it's heroic, but because it's carried out beneath the stars.

Secondly, I conjectured, because Kent was an artist working on flat surfaces, he sought, like every such artist, ways to suggest volume, to make the third dimension apparent. Beyond what clouds provide, the daytime sky has no depth; it's the night sky that gives an artist volume. While it takes an extraordinary person—the light and space artist James Turrell, say—to make the celestial vault visible in sunshine, many artists have successfully conveyed a sense of the sky's volume by painting it at night.

The conceit can easily grow up in a photographer that he or she has pretty much seen all the large things—the range of possible emotion to be evoked with light, the contrasts to be made by arranging objects in different scales, problems in the third and fourth dimension. But every serious photographer, I believe, has encountered at some point ideas unanticipated and dumbfounding. The shock causes you to reexamine all you've assumed about your own work and the work of others, especially the work of people you've never particularly understood. This happened most recently for me in seeing the photography of Linda Connor. While working on a story about international air freight, I became so disoriented, flying every day from one spot on the globe to another thousands of miles away, I did not know what time I was living in. Whatever time it was, it was out of phase with the sun, a time not to be dialed up on a watch, mine or anyone else's.

At a pause in this international hurtling, during a six-hour layover in Cape Town, I went for a ride with an acquaintance. He drove us out to Clifton Bay on the west side of Table Mountain. I was so dazed by my abuse of time that I was open to thoughts I might otherwise never have had. One of those thoughts was that I could recognize the physicality of time. We can discern the physical nature of space in a picture, grasp the way, for example, Robert Adams is able to photograph the air itself, making it visible like a plein air painter. In Cape Town that day I saw what I came to call indigenous time. It clung to the flanks of Table Mountain. It resisted being absorbed into my helter-skelter time. It seemed not yet to have been subjugated by Dutch and British colonial expansion, as the physical landscape so clearly had been. It was time apparent to the senses, palpable. What made me believe I was correct in this perception was that, only a month before, I'd examined a collection of Linda Connor's work, a book called *Luminance.* I realized there at Table Mountain that she'd photographed what I was looking at. She'd photographed indigenous time.

I'd grasped Ms. Connor's photographs in some fashion after an initial pass, but I hadn't sensed their depth, their power, what Gerard Manley Hopkins called "the achieve of the thing." With this new insight I wrote her an excited note, an attempt to thank her for work that opened the door to a room I'd never explored.

One of the great blessings of our modern age, a kind of redemption for its cruelties and unmitigated greed, is that one can walk down to a corner bookstore and find a copy of Ms. Connor's book. Or of Robert Adams's *What We Brought: The New World,* or Frans Lanting's *Bonobo: The Forgotten Ape,* or, say, Mary Peck's *Chaco Canyon: A Center and Its World,* and then be knocked across the room by a truth one had not, until that moment, clearly discerned.

It is more than illumination, though, more than a confirmation of one's intuition, aesthetics, or beliefs that comes out of the perusal of such a photographer's images. It's regaining the feeling that one is not cut off from the wellsprings of intelligence and goodwill, of sympathy for human plight.

I do not know, of course, why the photographers I admire, even the ones I know, photograph, but I am acutely aware that without the infusion of their images hope would wither in me. I feel an allegiance to their work more as a writer than as someone who once tried to see in this way, perhaps because I presume we share certain principles related to the effort to imagine or explain.

It is correct, I think, as Robert Adams wrote me that

day, to believe in a community of artists stimulated by and respectful of one another's work. But it's also true that without an audience (of which we're all a part) the work remains unfinished, unfulfilled. A photographer seeks intimacy with the world and then endeavors to share it. Inherent in that desire to share is a love of humanity. In different media, and from time to time, we have succeeded, I believe, in helping one another understand what is going on. We have come to see that, in some way, this is our purpose with each other.

FLIGHT

One foggy January morning in 1977, a few hours before dawn, a DC-8 freighter crashed on takeoff at Anchorage International Airport, killing all five people aboard and fifty-six head of cattle bound for Tokyo. Rescuers found the white-faced Herefords flung in heaps through the thick, snowy woods, their bone-punctured bodies, dimly lit by kerosene fires, steaming in the chill air.

A few days after the accident I happened to land in Anchorage on a flight from Seattle, en route to Fairbanks. The grisly sight of the wreck and the long scar ripped through birch trees off the end of the runway made me philosophical about flying. Beyond the violent loss of human life, it was some element of innocence in the cattle I kept coming back to. Were they just standing there calmly in large metal pens when the plane crashed? And why were they needed in Tokyo? At 35,000 feet over the winter Pacific, cruising that frigid altitude at 400 knots, did their lowing and jostle seem as bucolic?

Like many people who fly often, I have watched dozens of windowless air freighters lumbering by on taxiways and wondered at their cargos. In the years after that accident I puzzled over them everywhere—in Quito, in Beijing, in Nairobi, in Frankfurt, in Edmonton. What could warrant a fleet of machines so sophisticated and expensive to operate? It must be more than plasma and vaccines they haul, materials desperately needed; more than cut flowers, gold, and fruit, things highly valued or perishable. Would it be simply the objects people most desire? A fresh strawberry on a winter morning in Toronto?

Watching pallets go aboard on monotonously similar tarmacs around the world, I became more and more curious. I wanted to know what the world craved. I wanted a clarifying annotation for the rag-doll scatter of cattle.

At two a.m. one December night I climbed aboard a 747 freighter in Chicago to begin a series of flights around the world with freight.★ I would fly in and out of cities like Taipei, Rotterdam, and Los Angeles with drill pipe, pistol targets, frozen ostrich meat, lace teddies, dog food, digital tape machines, pythons, and ball caps; with tangerines from Johannesburg, gold bullion from Argentina, and orchid clusters from Bangkok. During the hourless penetration of space between continents, I would sidle among the eighty or more tons of airborne freight on the main deck, examining disparate labels like an inquiring bird.

★The forty flights, covering about 110,000 nautical miles, were made aboard 747 freighters and on 747 passenger planes hauling substantial amounts of cargo in their lower-deck compartments or, with some aircraft configurations, on the aft portion of the main deck, separated from the passengers by a bulkhead.

Out cockpit windows on the flight deck, I would become absorbed in the strange untapering stillness of the Earth seen from that altitude.

Before I boarded the first flight, however, I wanted to learn about the plane.

▌

The assembly building at Boeing's aircraft plant at Everett, Washington, is so large—ninety-eight acres under a single roof more than a hundred feet off the ground—that it has its own weather. Sometimes low clouds form in steelwork near the ceiling, where gantry cranes carrying subassembled sections of 747s, 767s, and 777s maneuver toward sites of final assembly. Over a single November night I watched swing-shift and third-shift crews at the plant complete the assembly of a 747-400 freighter, nearly the largest plane ever to fly. I studied it, and listened and touched, as its 68,000-pound wings were joined to a fuselage section, the six fuselage sections slid together and landing gear attached beneath, leaving it to tower above workers, empty as a cathedral, aloof as the moon.

As a boy I raised tumbler pigeons, a breed that at some height above the ground will destroy its aerodynamic lift and come plummeting down like a feathered stone, only to pull out at the very last moment, a terrifying demonstration of power and grace. Model airplanes—P-47, P-38, F-86, B-29—hung from the ceiling of my bedroom on black thread; I was mesmerized by the wind seething in eucalyptus trees around the house. Once I leaped hopefully from our roof with an open umbrella.

At seventeen I entered college as an aeronautical engineer, only to discover it was the metaphors of flight, not its mechanics, that moved me. I was less interested in engineering than in the imagination of an Antoine de Saint-Exupéry, who wrote of the "tender muslin of the meadows, the rich tweed of the woods," who climbed into the open cockpit of his Sahara-bound mail plane with heavy clothes and a tool bag, like a deep-sea diver, and who died in a crash in the Mediterranean in a P-38, a plane my mother's first husband helped design.

I switched to liberal arts, but the marvel of airborne flight never diminished for me. And the exotic allure of the Earth continued to tug. I saw the sky as an airscape of winds—West Africa's *harmattan,* Greece's damp *Apeloites,* California's Santa Ana, Japan's *daiboufu* ("the wind that knocks horses down").

I admired what I saw come tangibly together that night in the Boeing assembly building: a staggering achievement in engineering, in metallurgy, in economy of design. The assembly of a 747-400 freighter—232 feet long, 165 tons poised over eighteen tires like a barefoot gymnast on a balance beam, a six-story drop from the apex of its tail to the ground—suggests the assembly of a chronometer by tweezer, a sculptor's meaning with a jeweler's fastidiousness. Standing on a scaffold inside a wheel well, I marveled at a set of brass-colored steel screws securing six hydraulic lines in a pattern neat as a musical staff. Not a tool mark, not a misstep was to be seen. (Elsewhere, workers were buffing the airplane's aluminum skin to remove scratches I couldn't find with the pads of my fingers.) Fuselage sections came together smooth as a cap sliding onto a French fountain pen.

For twelve or thirteen hours that night I watched, wandering off to sift through a box of button-head rivets (three million of the plane's six million parts were rivets); or to observe agile men disappearing into the labyrinthine recesses of another 747's unfinished wing; or to heft "nuclear hardened" cable—flexible, shielded conduit that carries thick bundles of color-coded wire from controls on the flight deck to each engine. Then I circled back to the freighter—this particular one being built for Singapore Airlines—with another bit of understanding, a new appreciation of its elegance. People who saw the 747's first flight, in 1969, were impressed that something so huge could fly. What surprised the pilots was its nimbleness, its fluid response to their foot and hand pressures, the easy way the aircraft absorbed turbulence. Designing a plane to fly this well is exceedingly difficult. The engineering task, the working out of that single genetic code, proves to be beyond the reach of formulas. It's as intuitive and mysterious a process—and as prone to catastrophe—as developing and holding on to the financial market for such things.

The Boeing 747 is the one airplane every national airline strives to include in its fleet, to confirm its place in modern commerce, and it's tempting to see it as the ultimate embodiment of what our age stands for. Superficially, it represents an apotheosis in structural engineering and in the applied use of exotic metals and plastics. Its avionics and electronics systems incorporate all the speed and design efficiency of modern communications, and in terms both of manufacturing and of large-scale corporate organization, the swift assembly of its millions of parts is a model of streamlining and integration. In the air, the object itself is a virtuoso solution to flight, to Icarus's dream of escape and freedom. It operates with as little regard for geography, weather, political boundaries, intimidating physical distance, and time as anything humans have ever devised.

If subtleties in the plane's engineering were beyond my understanding, the spare grace of its long lines was not, nor its utilitarian perfection. The only thing that disturbed it, I was told, were rogue winds, the inevitable riptides and flash floods of the troposphere.

When I measured off the freighter's nearly completed main deck that night—sixty-eight paces down the bare interior—I was thinking of the quintessential symbol of another era, the Gothic cathedral of twelfth-century Europe, and of its emptiness, which we once filled with religious belief. Standing on the main deck, above the boxlike stub that joins the wing roots, standing where "nave" meets "transept" and looking up toward the pilots' "chancel," I recalled the intention behind Lúcio Costa's Brasília, a fresh city, aligned east and west like a cathedral but laid out in the shape of an airplane. But there on the assembly line the issue of spirituality, as serious a consideration as blood in the veins of a people, remained vague. The machine was magnificent, beautiful as staggered light on water, complex as an insoluble murmur of quadratic equations. But what placed within it could compare with religious faith?

In the assembly building that night, the 747 came together so quickly that to be away even for half an hour

meant missing lines in a sketch that soon became a painting. I would stand in one place, then another amid the
cocoon of jigs, cradles, floor jacks, elevated walkways, and
web slings surrounding the plane, watching while teams of
men, some in sleeveless shirts with ponytails and tattoos,
polished off a task neat as a snap of dry fingers in slow
motion. They were glad for the work. They knew it could
disappear in a trice, depending on the banks, the market, a
securities trader in Singapore.★

An aircraft will give away some of its character to a slow
walk-around. If you stare nose-on at a 747, you can tell
whether the plane is fueled or not by the angle at which
the wings sag. Empty, they assume an upward dihedral,
making the plane appear to rest even more lightly on its
wheel trucks. This vertical flexibility in the wings partly
explains the sensation of unperturbed agility one feels as a
passenger. If you let your eye run to the tip of either wing,
you can see another key: a slight horizontal twist apparent
in the last thirty feet or so, an engineer's quick, intuitive
solution to damping a troublesome oscillation. A similar
intuition once compelled Wilbur Wright to warp the lead-
ing edge of the wings of an experimental glider, lending it

★As a singular icon the 747 also symbolizes huge economic risk, brutal financial efficiency, and despotic corporate ego. Boeing president William Allen and
Pan American's Juan Trippe dared each other to take the then mind-boggling
steps of building and contracting for the 747. Who would go first? In 1969,
when Boeing's total debt after developing the plane was thought to be larger
than its net worth, it eliminated sixty thousand jobs to save the company, pushing Seattle's unemployment to 17 percent.

critical lateral stability. The glider metamorphosed into *Flyer,* in which, on December 17, 1903, at Kill Devil Hills on the North Carolina coast, Orville Wright achieved powered, sustained, controllable flight for the first time.

During the evening that I studied the buildup of the Singapore Airlines freighter, I was prompted, often, to reflect on early aviation. The vast interior of the Boeing plant and the peculiar absence of industrial noise combined to make the distant movement of messengers riding vintage bicycles seem almost timeless. The sight of these parts couriers gliding across the smooth concrete floors on fifties-era Schwinns triggered thoughts about the bicycle-building Wright brothers. The written history of all that led up to that December morning in 1903 reveals two young men who, beyond anything else, wanted to fly, at a time when most others were keen simply on winning the prize that feat would earn. While other people threw contraptions at the air, the Wright brothers worked out in painstaking detail the first practicable formulas for flight, challenging the previously revered mathematics of a German glider pilot named Otto Lilienthal, the author of *Birdflight as the Basis of Aviation* (1889). When *Flyer* flew, with its cambered wing and controllable elevator, its rudder and the world's first rudimentary ailerons, the Wright brothers knew exactly what they were doing. The achievement at Kill Devil Hills was not the fact that the plane sustained itself at about seven miles per hour over 120 feet, or the addition of a motor and props to a glider, but that Orville controlled it. He *flew* the plane.

The Wrights' entrepreneurial success embodies for many a vanquished innocence in America: this was an unprecedented thing, done for love, with little thought of personal gain, and financed largely out-of-pocket.

Orville's initial flight carried him about half the length of a 747 freighter's main deck. He was airborne for twelve seconds in a craft stripped of every bit of excess weight. The plane I was standing beside that night can carry 122 tons 5,000 nautical miles in about ten hours. The Wright brothers had little inkling of commercial advantage; without the support of government subsidies and the promise of private profit, without corporations competing fiercely for shares in a marketplace, without continuous turnover in what's considered fashionable in consumer goods, the 747 freighter might easily have gotten no further than a draftsman's table.

My last impression of the plane, the rainy morning I drove away, was of accomplishment. Whatever people might do with it, however they might fill this empty vessel, it gleamed to my way of thinking like an ideal. It was an exquisite reification of the desire for beauty.

Sometime later, I returned to Everett to inspect the finished cockpit. I wanted to crawl into every space that would admit me: low, tight bays on either side of the nose-wheel doghouse that hold tiers of maintenance computers; the transverse avionics bay aft of them, where the plane's triple-redundant inertial navigation system and flight deck computers are located (and from where, via hatches above and below, one can either drop to the tarmac or emerge on the main deck). I wanted to orient myself among banks of Halon bottles (the fire-fighting system) and emergency oxygen tanks on the lower cargo deck. I wanted to enter the compartment aft of the rear pressure bulkhead and see the massive jackscrew that tilts the horizontal stabilizer (the fins that protrude like a rear wing from the plane's tail).

Once the plane was fitted with four Pratt & Whitney engines—each developing up to 56,000 pounds of thrust (about 21,000 horsepower)—Singapore Airlines would take it away. At something like $155 million, it was an enormous capital investment; but with an international airfreight market currently expanding at about three times the rate of the passenger market, Boeing's plane number RR835 would soon pay for itself. After that, grossing upward of $750,000 per load against an operating cost of roughly $15,000 per hour, it would begin to earn its owners a substantial and unencumbered profit.

III

After Frankfurt's Rheim/Main Airport and London's Heathrow, Amsterdam's Schiphol International Airport is Europe's largest airfreight depot site. KLM's operation here is efficient and organized—dangerous goods here, live animals there, valuables (jewelry, currency, silver bars, uncut gemstones) over here, drugs in yet another place. In this world "perishable," I learned right away, refers to more than flowers, food, and newspapers; it includes everything in tenuous fashion: watches, video games, shades of lipstick, a cut of trouser—objects for which a few days' head start on store shelves is crucial.

On an upper half-floor of the cavernous outbound-freight building—the main floor includes an open space perhaps 600 by 200 feet, and 40 feet high—there is no one, only automated equipment, enslaved by a computerized sorting program that is updated continually in response to aircraft schedule changes and new delivery priorities. The loaders, moving on floor tracks, pull standard-size pallets and cargo containers from steel shelves at just the right moment to launch them on a path terminating promptly at the cargo doors of their intended airplane. It is stark, bloodless work. On the main floor the mechanical tedium is relieved in three ways: in the buildup of single pallets, with workers arranging dozens of small packages trimly in an eight-by-ten-foot-square load, at heights to fit either the upper or lower deck of a particular aircraft, and with one top edge rounded slightly to conform to the curve of the plane's sidewall; by the loading of oddly shaped or remarkable objects—a matched set of four, dark blue Porsche 911s, a complete prefabricated California ranch-style house; and by the sheer variety of goods—bins of chilled horsemeat, Persian carpets, diplomatic mail bound in sisal twine and sealed with red wax, bear testicles, museum art exhibits, cases of explosives.

The impression one gets amid tiers of briefly stored cargo and whizzing forklifts is of mirthless haste. A polite but impatient rectitude about the importance of commerce prevails, and it forestalls simple questions: Have they run out of mechanical pencils in Houston? Is the need for eelpout in Osaka now excruciating? Are there no more shirtmakers in Rangoon?

The following day I departed the freezing rain and spitting snow of Amsterdam for Cape Town, six thousand miles and an opposing season to the south, where one of KLM's smallest facilities operates on a decidedly different scale. We came in by way of Johannesburg and brought, among other things, two Goeldi's marmosets and eight white ear-tufted marmosets, both endangered, inbound from South America for a local attraction called Monkey Den.

When my escort completed our tour—a semienclosed metal shed, no automation—he very kindly suggested we go for a drive. He felt harried by shippers' phone calls, cajoling for more space than he could provide on the outbound flight. I, too, wanted to get away from the clamor.

For the past six days I had been flying a heavy schedule, mostly in and out of the Far East. I was bewildered by the speed with which everything moved, by how quickly I came and went through the countries. In a few hours I would turn around and fly back to Johannesburg, there to pick up fresh flowers, hunting trophies, and raw diamonds before returning to wintry Amsterdam.

We drove east through windblown sand scrub on the Cape Flats, rather quickly through Cape Town itself, and around to Clifton Bay on the west side of Table Mountain. The weather had been hot, but it was cooler now, seventy-two, with a brisk southeast wind, the one they call the Doctor.

For a long while I stood there on the bluff in the summer sunshine, staring into the transparent blue water of the Atlantic. I was acutely aware of history here at Bartolemeu Dias's Cabo Tormentoso (the Portuguese navigator's Cape of Storms, a foreboding appellation his king would later change to Cabo da Bõa Esperança, Cape of Good Hope). Cook and Darwin anchored here as did, in 1522, a rem-

nant of that part of Magellan's crew under Sebastián del
Cano. In those days it had taken as many months as it now
takes hours to come this far south from Europe, and an
indifferent sea swamped and crushed the Dutch *jachts* and
Iberian caravels like a child's paper sailers. Robben Island,
where Nelson Mandela spent so many years, was just to the
north. A few miles to the southeast was Skildergat Cave, a
35,000-year-old early human site. All this was once the
landscape of the Khoikhoi people, now long since gone to
Namibia and Botswana, where they are called San people
and among whom are the much studied !Kung.

My companion was speaking English with a friend.
When he lapsed into Afrikaans I recalled how, over the past
few days, I had been scrambling to get the simplest grasp of
Malay, Thai, then Hindi. I was moving carelessly around
the planet. Beneath the familiar jet lag I began to sense
something else: physical geography was not only spatial, it
was temporal. I looked up past my shoulder at the serene
oak and pine forests of Table Mountain, da Gama's defining pivot. It had a peculiar time to it, as indigenous as its
rock. I could not take that time with me, nor bring my
own time here and drape it possessively over the mountain.
In that moment I glimpsed the impunity with which I was
traveling, as well as the inseparability of time and space in
geography. The dispensation I enjoyed from the historical
restraints of immense distance had created an illusion
about time: the Earth's spaces might vary terrifically—the
moonlight reflecting for me last night on Shatt Al-Meghir,
a saline lake in barren eastern Algeria, was not the same
moonlight shining back from the icy reaches of Cook Inlet

in Anchorage—but time, until this moment, had seemed a seamless thing, never qualitatively different. Everywhere I went time continued the same, an imperial present. At most, in these new depots and their environs, I was resetting my watch.

As I stood there gazing at Table Mountain, then back at the transparent Atlantic, I knew the mountain's time was not my time. And that I would not, now, give in to its time. I was on this other, no-Sunday, no-night, on-time, international commercial time. I sought out my friend and asked, "Shouldn't we be getting back?" I was starting to behave as if the present were only a preparation for the future. When I phoned my wife from some point along the way to confide that I was deeply bewildered, that it was as though all the rests in a symphony score had become threats, she said, "It's because you're not going anywhere, you're just going."

Two changes in the late eighties boosted the growth of international airfreight. Up until then shipping by air meant being assured your goods would arrive at such-and-such an airport within forty-eight hours of a promised time. Today, for an average of one to four dollars a pound, a customer expects guaranteed, on-time delivery; and increasingly that service is door-to-door, not airport-to-airport. The largest airfreight operation in the world (though the bulk of what they haul is small packets) is Federal Express. Next, in descending order of tonnage carried, are Lufthansa, UPS, and Air France, then Korean Air and Singapore. (At present, profitability in the industry remains marginal while airlines continue to maneuver for market share.)

Most air cargo, according to an industry forecaster, now consists of "high-value, time-perishable, consumer items." The business is driven by three things: the growing expectation, worldwide, of having whatever one wants tomorrow, not next week or next month; by frequent changes in fashion and in the design of basic products; and by a great disparity in labor costs from one country to the next. Much of what one sees aboard a freighter is placeless merchandise; except for the cost of employing a person, it might have been manufactured almost anywhere, including the country of destination. A museum director in Los Angeles found it less expensive, for example, to have the museum's entire red sandstone façade quarried in India, air-freighted to Japan to be dressed, and then flown to Los Angeles than to have it quarried, dressed, and trucked in from Minnesota.

Companies ship city phone books from the United States to China to have the names inexpensively keyed in on mailing lists. Automobile insurance claims travel by the boxful from Miami to Manila to be processed by people who are not only cheaper to employ but who make fewer mistakes than the clerks for hire in Miami. And air shippers, exploiting the same small margins currency traders use, find it less costly to have, say, nine tons of rayon blouses machine-cut in Hong Kong and flown to Beijing to be finished by hand than to have all the work done in Hong Kong—before the blouses are flown on to customers in Berlin or Chicago.

On long eight- and ten-hour trips on the freighters, I

regularly left the flight deck, though it seemed always to be offering me some spectacular view of the Earth—Mt. Pinatubo smoldering in the depopulated Zambales Mountains on Luzon, or L'Anse aux Meadows, a bleak site on the northern tip of Newfoundland where Norse people established a community about A.D. 1000. Leaving these, I'd climb down the narrow, folding aluminum stairs and stroll the aisles at the perimeter of the cargo load. Containerized or shrink-wrapped in heavy plastic, tagged with routing labels in code, the shipments were frequently difficult to identify without the help of manifests or air waybills. One night out of Taipei: 17 cartons of basketballs for Boston; 5,898 pounds of sunglasses headed for Atlanta; 85 cartons of women's polyester pajamas for Columbus, Ohio; cameras, men's ties, battery-operated action-hero toys; 312 pounds of wristwatches for New York. What I saw very often seemed the fulfillment of mail-order-catalog dreams. The celerity in airfreight, in fact, and the freighter's ability to gather and distribute goods over huge distances in a matter of hours, have made the growth of 800-number stores like J. Crew, Lands' End, and Victoria's Secret possible. By promoting "just in time" delivery—neither a sweater, a comic book, nor a jet engine arrives until the moment it's needed—freight companies have also (1) changed the way businesses define inventory, (2) made it possible for stores to turn storage space into display space, and (3) forced governments to reconsider the notion of an inventory tax.

What planes fly, generally, is what people imagine they want. Right now.

Back at D. F. Malan International Airport in Cape Town, I watched a six-man crew load freight—Cape wines, salted snook headed for New York fish counters, 3,056 pounds of ostrich meat bound for Brussels, one Wheaton terrier named Diggs for Toronto.

Standing there on the ramp, I asked my companion if he knew about the first shipment of airfreight, in 1910. No, he didn't. It was 542 square yards of silk, I said, carried sixty miles from Dayton to Columbus, Ohio. It cost Morehouse-Martens of Columbus $5,000, but they made a profit of more than $1,000 by cutting the fabric up into small pieces and selling them as souvenirs to customers at their dry-goods store.

He told me the fellow shipping ostrich meat, frustrated by a lack of cargo space out of Cape Town, had a restaurant in California interested, but without the space he couldn't close the deal. We were looking, at that moment, at the aircraft I had come in on, a 747-400 passenger plane with about 5,900 cubic feet of lower-hold cargo space (passenger baggage might take up only 20 percent of this). Depending on the demand for seating, KLM might occasionally fly a 747-400 Combi into Cape Town. In this aircraft, the aft section on the main deck is given over to seven pallets of freight, while passengers are seated in the forward section—an efficient way for airlines to take advantage of fluctuations in both passenger and freight markets.

Tons of fish, he said, let alone more ostrich meat, could be shipped from Cape Town, if only he could guarantee his customers the room. Today he'd be happy to squeeze a surfboard into the bulk-cargo hold, the space farthest aft on the lower deck, a last-on, first-off, loose-loaded compartment, where mail, air waybills, crew baggage, and, today, the Wheaton terrier went. We continued to exchange stories about peculiar things one sees on board—a yacht headed for an America's Cup race; a tropical-hardwood bowling alley from Bangkok; in San Francisco enough boxed Bing cherries, tied three to a bunch and packed neat as flashlight batteries, to fill one 747 freighter after another (27,000 cubic feet). They're not supposed to, I said, but one of the pilots told me he liked to sit in the Ferraris and Lamborghinis he flew. "I've driven them many miles," the pilot mused, "and very fast."

Business was good, I told my guide, but strange. Two days before, on what pilots call the Tashkent Route between Europe and the cities of Karachi, Delhi, Bangkok, Singapore, and Jakarta (via Russia, Kazakhstan, Uzbekistan, and Afghanistan, because the Himalayas are too high and Iranian airspace too dangerous), I had seen rocket fire and streams of tracer ammunition in Kabul, Taliban "extremists" and their entrenched opponents. People were being shot dead below, but to the east a full moon was rising rapidly, orange and huge as the sun. It silhouetted sharply the sawtooth peaks of southern ranges in the Hindu Kush. And farther to the southeast, beyond the Khyber Pass and high above the Indus River, a hundred miles of lightning bolts flared and jangled along a storm front. With one glance I took it all in: rockets flaming across the streets below, the silent moon, rain falling in the Indus Valley from a ceiling of cloud, above which the black vault of the sky glittered with stars.

On the Tashkent Route, I continued, air-traffic controllers in Dushanbe, Tajikistan, pass you on to Lahore, skipping
chaotic Kabul altogether. Their voices crackle on the high-
frequency radio like explosions of glass, trilling aviation
English in the high-pitched intonation of a muezzin. At
Lahore, you can see the Pakistani border stretching away
north into the Punjab, a beaded snake of security lighting.
From here west all the way to Libya (whose air-traffic controllers reprimand careless pilots that it is not "Libya" but
"Libyan Arab Jamahiriyah Territory"), religious and political tension is pointedly apparent from the sky. Coming up
from Dubai, we would swing far out to the west, over Saudi
Arabia, to fly wide of Iraq, then dogleg north across Jordan,
staying to the east of Israel. Leaving Lebanon's skies, we'd
enter disputed airspace over eastern Cyprus. Greek Cypriot
and Turkish Cypriot air-traffic controllers do not play dangerous games with commercial aircraft, but, together with
the Syrians, they contest the right among themselves to assign
you flight levels and headings. Once across Turkey we'd bear
north to stay wide of Bosnia-Herzegovina.

Every pilot I spoke with, I said to the young KLM
freight manager, had a story of the white-orange flash of
lethal fighting seen from above, the named and unnamed
wars of the modern era, fought in Timor, in the Punjab, in
what were once called the lawless hinterlands, but which
are now as accessible as Detroit or Alice Springs.

On the return flight from Cape Town to Johannesburg, I
glanced through data comparing this 747-400 with others

in KLM's fleet.★ Each 747, despite being built to the same specifications and being fitted with the same engines, consistently burns slightly more or less fuel, or "performs differently against the book." Northwest Airlines flies eight 747-200 freighters into the Far East; I flew on four of them, trying to gain a feeling for their personalities. (With so much history, distance, and weather, I reasoned—so many minor accidents, replaced engines, and strange cargos—there had to be personality.) Once I stayed with a single aircraft through five crew changes, from Hong Kong to Tokyo, then on to Anchorage, Chicago, and New York before turning back for Seattle—in all about 12,000 nautical miles in 56 hours. Reading the plane's operating certificates (posted on a lavatory bulkhead in the cockpit) and its logbooks, and poking into all its accessible spaces, what I found was distinctiveness, not personality.

It was 2:30 in the morning and raining when we landed in Seattle. After the dehydrating hours aloft, mildly hypoxic, my tissues swollen from undissolved nitrogen, I was glad for the wet, oxygen-rich air at sea level. With a security escort shifting idly from one foot to the other at my side, I drew the night air in deeply and brushed rain across my face. I'd been with the plane for so many hours—I periodically rolled a pad and sleeping bag out on the floor of the flight deck to sleep—that an uncomplicated affection had built up for all it had accomplished while the crews came

★Virtually all wide-body passenger aircraft carry a diverse and often substantial belly cargo of manufactured goods, flowers, fresh food, and live animals. With so many people now living and working abroad, they also commonly carry large containers of personal effects and the coffins of returning nationals.

and went. Its engines were silent now, still. I walked beneath it in the dim illumination from warehouse lights.

The freighter's belly—this plane was 6729F—was glazed with a thin oil film. In it, and in exhaust grime on the engines' housings, mechanics had finger-traced graffiti. (Inside, on cargo compartment walls, ground crews often scrawl insults—some of a sexual nature—aimed at ground crews in other cities. On inaccessible surfaces within the wings, I was told by riveters at the Boeing plant, some paint declarations of love.) I made a mental note to check 6729F's technical log, a sort of running medical history of the aircraft, to see when it had last been "A-B-C-Ded," a forty-day swarming by mechanics during which every structural part, every rivet, every wire, is examined or X-rayed.

The fifteen-year-old plane's thin (.063 inches) tempered aluminum skin was scraped and dented and it bore a half dozen aluminum patches. (In an effort to keep a plane on schedule, some of these minor tears are first repaired provisionally with "speed tape.") Its windows were micropitted, its 32-ply tires slightly worn, its livery paint chipped. Looking aft from a point near the turn of its flat, streaked belly, I realized the plane had the curved flanks of a baleen whale, in an identical scale, exact to the extended flukes of its horizontal stabilizer.

Overall the freighter had a lean, polished, muscular patina. It flew in the working world.

IV

I first flew with horses on another Northwest flight, out of Chicago's O'Hare on a bitterly cold February night.★ These sixteen were headed for lives on Hokkaido ranches among the well-to-do: a Percheron stallion; twelve Appaloosas, and three quarter horses, accompanied by two handlers.

We were delayed three hours getting out. The driver of one of the loaders, a steerable platform used to raise cargo fifteen feet to the rear cargo door, accidentally rammed the plane, punching a hole in a canoe fairing (a cover protecting the jackscrew that extends and retracts the plane's flaps, and which "fairs" or tapers this protrusion into the wing). We also had to replace an exhaust-gas temperature gauge on the number-three engine, the sort of maintenance that goes on regularly.

The pilot made a shallow climb out of Chicago to lessen the strain on the horses' back legs. He headed out over Wisconsin and Minnesota on a slight zigzag that would take us from one way point to another en route to Anchorage. Planes rarely fly a direct route between airports unless the skies are relatively empty, usually late at night, the time when most freight moves. Freighter pilots, some of whom wear bat wings on their tunics instead of eagle wings and

---

★Thoroughbred horses fly back and forth between the continents constantly during the respective national racing seasons. Slaughter horses, mostly young draft horses, are carried to the Far East from the United States and Canada, 116 head at a time in 29 pens on a 747. With a reduction in import duties on fresh meat in the Far East, smaller animals like the slaughter cattle killed in the Anchorage crash, have become less economical to fly live.

refer to themselves as "freight dogs," call it "flying the backside of the clock."

Soon after we're airborne I go down to look at the horses. The main deck temperature has been set at 55 degrees so I take a jacket. The animals are lined up in six stalls on the right side of the aircraft, the 2,100-pound black Percheron in the first stall with a bred quarter horse; behind them a leopard Appaloosa stallion with a bred Appaloosa; and behind them, downwind in the flow of air, four stalls of bred and "open" mares, with four fillies and colts. They aren't sedated, most are dozing. They've been left unshod to give them a better hold on the stall floor, and won't be watered or fed for twenty-four hours in transit. Hemmed in by the usual farrago—aortic valves, poultry-processing equipment, mainframe computers, golf clubs, men's knit underwear—the horses seem strangely peaceful. I can't hear their breathing or stomach noises over the sound of the engines. I turn the lights out and leave them be.

On the flight deck, a narrow space like a railway-car living room, the horse handlers are slumped with novels in a single row of three tourist-class seats toward the rear, the only three passenger seats available besides the jump seat. The flight engineer has just brewed a fresh pot of coffee. I settle in behind the captain to peruse the flight manifests. I gaze out the window. Every few minutes I look at the instrument panel in front of the copilot and at the hydraulic, fuel, and electrical panels in front of the flight engineer, sitting a few inches to my right.

The 747 is not the biggest freighter in the world, but in every other way—making long hauls economically on a scheduled basis—it is unrivaled. The biggest plane in regular service is the Russian Antonov 124, a fuel-guzzling, hulking beast of an aircraft that works at the fringes of the world of airfreight, hauling unusual loads on a charter basis. The only way to move emergency equipment (oil-skimming boats, fire-fighting trucks) or large quantities of emergency supplies (medicine, food, gas masks, cots) quickly around the world is on airfreighters, and the Antonov 124 ferries such material routinely, and many more unusual things: French fighter planes to Venezuela; 132 tons of stage equipment for a Michael Jackson concert in Bucharest; a Pepsi-Cola bottling plant, complete, to Buenos Aires; a 38-ton bull gear to repair an oil tanker stranded in the Persian Gulf; 36,000 cubic feet of cigarettes per flight on repeated trips between Amsterdam and Moscow during the breakup of the Soviet Union.

When we pass through 18,000 feet, the flight engineer sets our altimeters to read against an atmospheric pressure of 29.92 inches of mercury. We'll calibrate altitude against this pressure until we descend on approach into Anchorage, an agreed-upon standard that ensures planes all over the world will be figuring their altitudes on the same basis once they leave the airspace around an airport. We've also left local time behind. Now all our communications are based on Coordinated Universal Time (UTC), formerly Greenwich Mean Time or Zulu time, as it is still sometimes called (the Earth's time zones having once been divided among the letters of the alphabet). Another universal grid we are fixed in is degrees and minutes of latitude and longitude. And altitude, of course. (The altimeter always shows altitude above mean sea level; if the altimeter reads 7,500 feet over Mexico City, you are 100 feet off the ground.)

These grids provide a common reference, and their uniformity makes flying safer; but there are dissenters around the globe, especially where time zones are concerned. Tonga, along with Russia's Chukotski Peninsula, insists on occupying a twenty-fifth time zone. When it's 12:15 Sunday morning in Tonga, it's 11:15 Friday night in Western Samoa, a few hundred miles to the northeast. And against UTC whole hours, central Australia stays on the half hour, Nepal keeps to a three-quarter hour, and Suriname adheres to ten minutes before the hour.*

Virtually everyone communicates over the radio in English, but it is often heavily accented English, and outside customary requests and responses, English is of limited use in areas like China or in what pilots call Sea Asia. Russian pilots, for their part, are unique in insisting on the use of meters per second instead of knots for airspeed, and on meters instead of feet for altitude. In addition, Russian commercial planes don't use the Traffic Collision Avoidance System, which warns of approaching aircraft; nor do they send out a signal so planes with that system will know

---

*It is largely forgotten today that the notion of "standard time" in the United States, as opposed to local time, was one promulgated by railroad commissions to coordinate the needs of railroads and other businesses engaged in long-distance commerce. A nationwide system, enforced by railroads and then by factories, was entrenched by 1883. Congress eventually gave its official approval, though several states—Utah, Minnesota, California—fought the inconvenience until 1917. The principal objection was that standard time distorted the natural rhythms of human life for the sake of greater efficiency in business and commerce. Today Cincinnati lives, more or less complacently, by Boston's sunrise.

they're there. To politely register their disapproval of these tenuous arrangements, European pilots flash their landing lights at approaching Russian planes (which air-traffic controllers have alerted them are there) and wait for a response.

The wide acceptance of such standardized measurements and procedures can lead to the impression that a generally convivial agreement obtains throughout the world. And when, in one week, you transport the same sorts of freight to Cairo, Melbourne, and Rio de Janeiro, it is also easy to draw the conclusion that people everywhere want more or less the same things. However pervasive, the view is illusory. The airplane's speed and geographic reach benefit the spread of a European and North American consumer ethic, but not all the world's cultures can be folded into this shape. One need only leave the airport in Lima or Calcutta or Harare to see how true this is. It is not merely poverty and starvation you see, the ringing of another music you hear, or inversions of Western intuition you observe. It is starkly different renderings of the valuable.

Again and again, stalled in boulevard traffic in hot, choking air, feeling the taxi bumped by a languid crosscurrent of beggars, I thought of the speed of the plane, how much it could leave behind. If we fled quickly enough, I thought, nothing would catch up.

One morning at KLM's corporate headquarters in Amsterdam, I spoke with a vice president in his corner office. Beyond us, planes were taking off every couple of minutes like salvos. "When I was a boy," he said, "I was given my father's watch. I thought that would be my watch for the rest of my life. But I have five watches now. I choose one in the morning to match my suit, a tie. You just buy them."

He spread his hands, a gesture of lament and consternation. In an adjacent office, another vice president told me, "Speed is the word. Air cargo is the answer to speed, it makes speed happen." I could not tell from his piercing look whether he meant it as a summary or an indictment.

An oceanic expanse of pre-dawn gray white below obscures a checkered grid of Saskatchewan, a snow plain nicked by the dark, unruly lines of woody swales. One might imagine that little is to be seen from a plane at night, but above the clouds the Milky Way is a dense, blazing arch. A full moon often lights the planet freshly, and patterns of human culture, artificially lit, are striking in ways not visible in daylight. One evening I saw the distinctive glows of Bhiwani, Rohtak, Ghaziabad, and a dozen other cities around Delhi diffused like spiral galaxies in a continuous deck of stratus clouds far below us. In Algeria and on the Asian steppes, wind-whipped pennants of gas flared. The jungle burned in incandescent spots on peninsular Malaysia and in southern Brazil. One clear evening at 20,000 feet over Manhattan, I could see, it seemed, every streetlight halfway to the end of Long Island, as far east as Port Jefferson. A summer lightning bolt once unexpectedly revealed thousands of bright dots on the ink-black veld of the northern Transvaal: sheep. Another night, off the eastern coast of Korea, I arose from a nap to see a tight throw of the brightest lights I'd ever observed. I thought we were low over a city until I glanced at the horizon and saw the pallid glow of coastal towns between Yŏngdŏk and Samch'ŏk. The lights directly below, brilliant as magnesium flares, were those of a South Korean fishing fleet.

Over Anchorage we slam into severe turbulence at 34,000 feet. The plane seems suddenly to shrink, and we are pitched through the sky like a wood chip for ten minutes before we get clear of it and divert to Fairbanks. When I go below with a handler, the horses appear to have come through the violence unfazed. The handler knows each of the animals and speaks soothingly to them. As we proceed down the line, he recalls their breeding histories. Draft horses like the Percheron, he says, are the calmest breeds, and working quarter horses are bred for calmness. He isn't surprised they're all right, or that they settle down quickly.

If you ask pilots which loads they most remember, they mention either costly objects—a $319,000 Bentley, flying 70,000 pounds of gold into Riyadh—or animals, the things that are animated in a freight shipment. Most say Vietnamese potbelly pigs are the worst creatures to haul, their stench so permeating that pilots have to strip off their uniforms, seal them in plastic bags, and fly in clothes that they later throw away. As bad, they say, is a planeload of durians, a pulpy, melon-size fruit whose scent reminds most Western people of vomit. A problem that occurs on some cattle flights turns on their rank perspiration. Rising as a vapor, it penetrates the ceiling insulation and freezes to the plane's interior skin surfaces. Melted by warmer outside temperatures at lower altitudes on descent, the fluid funnels forward and begins dripping on the pilots.

When large animals—draft horses and bulls—kick their stalls in midflight, you can feel the plane shudder. Goats and ostriches will chew at whatever cargo they can reach. One pilot told me about going down one night to look at a white tiger. Believing she'd been sedated, he drew close to the bars to peer in. She charged as ferociously as the cage permitted, sending the pilot reeling onto his back. The animal's roar, he said, drowned out the sound of the engines and nearly stopped his heart.

Pilots remember animals in some detail—wolf puppies turned loose in the cockpit, a killer whale in a tank— because they are alive and making these formidable journeys. Like the pilots.

We wait in Fairbanks until the Anchorage weather quiets and then fly back, landing in light turbulence. A 747 freighter taking off just after we land hits a wind shear and in less than two seconds accelerates from 210 to 260 knots. An hour later, on takeoff, we abruptly lose 20 knots of airspeed when a headwind collapses. We're barely airborne when the departure threshold on the runway passes under our wheels. Two hours later our automatic pilot malfunctions. The nose plunges violently and we are in a rapid descent. In one of the most assured and swiftest moves I've ever seen a human being make, the pilot recovers the plane and brings it back level before we fall 500 feet.

When I again accompany the handlers below, we find the horses awakened by the fall and spooked by our soundless approach. They glare a while, then doze off. The rich odors in their corrals don't drift up to the flight deck. I thought they might, and take the edge of indifference off the electronic atmosphere up there.

In those same minutes the sun had just risen (at 30,000 feet it clears the horizon about twenty-two minutes earlier than it does when seen from a spot on the Earth directly below), but the moon had not yet set, and for a while I held both in the same gaze, in a sky that goes from azure to milk blue between horizons. We are pushing against a 120-knot headwind, common this time of year over the North Pacific. When I ask whether the pilots have names for these winds aloft around the world, the captain says, "No, we haven't been flying long enough." I ask whether the jet stream— "the jets," they call these winds—blows strongest here. Yes, he answers, here and over the North Atlantic. By then the copilot has located something he's been searching for in his personal logbook. On this same route last year, he shows me, headed the other way with a tailwind, he made the fastest ground speed he's experienced in a 747—702 knots.

Far beneath us the winds are calmer. The burnished surface of the ocean seven miles below appears still as a slab of stone, and crinkled like an elephant's skin. I see only one ship headed southwest against the Okhotsk Current, far off the coast of Kamchatka, its wake flared at the characteristic 39-degree angle.

When Japan looms I feel suddenly very tired. I haven't slept for thirty hours—traveling to Chicago, then caught up in events surrounding the horses, anticipating en route to Anchorage an appearance of the aurora borealis, listening to the pilots tell stories, looking out the window at the remoteness of Alaska, at the spectacle of clouds. Beneath us, every day, I'd seen buttermilk, mare's tail, and mackerel skies, and then looked in vain through phrase books and small dictionaries for what they are called in Korean, in Spanish.

We touch down at Narita International Airport at 12:42 p.m. local standard time. At 12:45 we set the plane's parking brake at Gate 211.* At 12:54 Japanese officials open the door and a quarantine officer boards to inspect the horses. Once he is assured of their good health, he leads us down the air stairs where, one by one, we step gingerly through a plastic basin of disinfectant. The horse handlers, wearing fine-looking Western boots, hesitate a moment.

The wood stalls are to be burned. The horses will be in quarantine here for three weeks before being flown to Hokkaido. I remember the snorts of steam and billowing breath on the frigid ramp at O'Hare and wish I could see them now, standing, like us, in the sunshine and balmy breezes outside the plane.

V

From my accustomed seat, just behind and slightly to the left of the pilot, I have a clear view to the southeast over the South China Sea. Though it is slightly awkward to manage, I often lean into this window. Just those few inches closer and my view widens appreciably. I look back at the port wing, the sleek gape of the winking engines, at a pinpoint of nuclear light winking on a windshield ten miles away. At night, if I rotate my head 180 degrees and hold the upper

---

*Pilots use different methods to compute their actual (as distinct from scheduled) flying time. One is "block to block," from the pulling of the nosewheel chocks at one end to their being set at the other end. Another is doors closed to doors open. Northwest pilots are limited, on this latter basis, to 82.5 hours of flying per month and to no more than 30 hours in any seven-day period.

edge of this canted window against the stars, the world is utterly still. We do not appear to move at all.

Far to the south, just now, a ribbon of sunlit cumulus towers, fumaroles and haystacks, great pompadour waves of this cloud. I never tire of seeing them, the most dominating evanescent form on the planet. We have seen a great range of them since leaving Tokyo some hours ago. East of Honshu, over the Pacific, the ocean was occluded by a vast sheet of wool-nap cumulus. When that flat plain opened into a lattice hundreds of miles later, the formation appeared serried in three dimensions, away from me and down. These puffs eventually thinned and I thought the sky cloudless until I looked up to see a rice-paper layer of cirrostratus. Then it, too, thinned to blue space, and for a while there was nothing but an occasional fair-weather cumulus, built up over a distant Pacific atoll, until we came to the rampart of heaped clouds—*cumulus congestus.* For all their beauty, the impossibly slow tai chi of their movement, clouds are of almost no help, claim the pilots, in anchoring a sense of depth or distance in the troposphere. They accentuate, however, the peculiar and insistent, ethereal nature of the sky.

I need to stretch. None of the three pilots wants anything from the galley,★ so I raise the smoke door (which

★The heritage of oceangoing vessels is preserved in the language and some of the design of modern airplanes. Pilots frequently call the plane a ship, its fuselage a hull. Its interior space is divided into decks that extend fore and aft. The captain might refer to starting an engine as turning a wheel. He steers the plane on the ground with a tiller and speaks of docking the ship, after which, on a freighter, cargo is always taken off the main deck on the port side (originally, the side of a ship designed for use in port). A rudder in the plane's vertical stabilizer changes its course. Waterline-like numbers stenciled on the interior of the fuselage indicate height above the ground. Sailboat fairings taper engine mounts into wings that bear green running lights to starboard, red lights to port.

would give us some protection in case of a main-deck fire)
and descend the stairs to take a turn around the cargo.
Unlike the pilots, I cannot resist a look each time the
plane's contents change. I am drawn by the promise of revelation in the main hold. "Used clothing" might mean a
boutique-consignment of East German military uniforms.
A persistent rumor of fabled cargo might be confirmed.*
The pilots, who speak animatedly about circus tigers, Lam-
borghini Diablos, and small wooden pallets of gold bars,
each in its own burlap bag, seem uninterested or vaguely
embarrassed by the bulk of what fills the space behind
their heads.†

The specter of a fire down here is, of course, terrifying,
as is the thought of a printing press or a stack of steel pipe
breaking loose in turbulence. For this reason the contents
of air shipments are carefully reviewed and documented;
pilots receive written notification of even the smallest
quantities of corrosives, explosives, and radioactive materials on board—anything that could start a fire. Cargo loads
are tightly secured and neatly arranged so as to be accessi-

---

*One story I heard many times but couldn't confirm concerned shipments of
large bluefin tuna to Japan from Newport, Rhode Island. A Newport buyer
with a small plane on standby reportedly offers returning sport fishermen a
premium price for any bluefin over 500 pounds. The fish is iced, flown immediately to JFK, and put aboard the first available commercial flight to Tokyo.

†About four a.m. one December night in Hong Kong, I stood at the top of
our air stairs scanning close-by office buildings with my binoculars. Decorated
Christmas trees twinkled on a dozen floors. I'd seen Christmas trees banked
with brightly wrapped gift boxes in Muslim Dubai and in the Buddhist city of
Bangkok, as well as in Amsterdam and Houston. The displays, of course, had
nothing to do with the Christianity of, say, Joseph of Arimathea. "This time of
year," one pilot told me while we waited for cargo in Hong Kong, "we're flying freighters out of here wingtip to wingtip."

ble in flight. The flight engineer's last responsibility on walk-around before departure is to check each piece of fire-fighting equipment and make sure that each pallet and container is secure; the ones I watched were thorough about it.

On flights to North America from the Far East's "new tigers"—Jakarta, Singapore, Bangkok, Hong Kong, Taipei—the planes ferried (in descending order, by weight) personal computers, sound-recording equipment, athletic shoes, photocopying equipment, and clothes. Traveling from North America to the Far East are comparable loads of motors and engines, personal computers, telecommunications equipment, and tractor parts. Such commodities formed the bulk of most shipments I accompanied, but it was the condiments, so to speak, that made a load memorable: two hundred Styrofoam cases of live tropical fish (labeled LTF), swimming in bags of oxygenated water, bound for Los Angeles from Manila; two Cadillac Eldorados—right-hand drive—for Osaka; canvas bags of homebound paper bills (the accumulation from currency exchanges); munitions of war (MUW) for Khartoum; bundles of mesquite wood, for restaurant cooking fires, out of Houston; and noisome industrial chemicals (OBX).

In a fully loaded 747-200, cargo is palletized on thin aluminum "cookie sheets," wrapped tightly in clear plastic weatherproofing (or opaque plastic, to discourage thieves), and secured against shifting on the pallet by webs or rope nets. Twenty-two rectangular sealed containers and pallets, dogged down to a floor of steel caster bearings and roller-track with red latches, stand in pairs down the middle of the freighter, leaving narrow outboard aisles. Two additional

units, canted to the taper of the plane, hug the starboard
wall into the nose. In the tail, aft of a ten-foot-wide cross
aisle directly opposite a cargo door, stand another four
units. A twenty-ninth unit, the last, stands behind them,
near the open wall rack that holds the plane's flight data
recorder and cockpit voice recorder (the "black boxes").

I sideslip past the containers and pallets on the port side
and look back from the cross aisle at the mass of our freight
for Singapore and Bangkok. It shimmies in the cobblestone
turbulence of what Wilbur Wright called "the infinite
highway of the air," a rickety but firm, continuous vibra-
tion. (From a viewport on the flight deck, with the area lit
dimly by only a few safety lights, the plastic-wrapped cargo
looks like a double row of huge jellyfish strung up in a
freezer.) I turn and clamber over the rearmost loads, reaching a white concave hemisphere marking the aft edge of
the main deck. Here, as far as possible from the plane's
compasses, is where any magnetized cargo is palletized.

Moving forward up the starboard aisle, I finally stand in
an eerie place, at the forward edge of the main deck, looking at the backside of the fiberglass radar dome that fills the
plane's nose. I look down into an open bay framed on
either side by large jackscrews which push the nose out and
up for loading through the front. The lip of this precipice,
which I grip with my toes, is as close as one can get to
standing on the bow of a ship. I spread my arms wide for
balance, shut my eyes, and lean into the velocity of the
plane. The sound of the engines is behind me, inaudible
over the scream of air.

———————

Chief pilots, or captains, men in their early fifties, "in the left-hand seat," tend to gaze to some purpose out the windows of the cockpit, while copilots, men (and, rarely, women), in their midthirties, remain focused within the plane.

In the evolution of modern jet flight, there has been a dramatic shift away from the use of navigation references outside the plane, such as rivers, to the use of electronically displayed information within the plane. Some of the copilots I spoke with, in fact, had only hazy notions of the geography they flew over. They were inclined to fly "heads down," studying a route map, reviewing the flight plan (a sequence of way points, an expected fuel burn, the speed and direction of winds aloft), and watching their instruments and display screens. On the most advanced commercial aircraft, it is the copilots who are frequently caught up in the protracted task of programming the plane's computers. ("I don't fly anymore," they joke, "but I can type sixty words a minute.")*

The chief pilots, many of them, possess a notable, unique knowledge of how the Earth has changed over the past thirty years; how much farther south the Sahara Desert has crept, how much the Aral Sea has shrunk, how far center-pivot irrigation has spread in Saudi Arabia. It's knowledge that predates satellite imagery and often is more historically integrated. Many of these pilots learned the Earth's surfaces when older planes held them to lower alti-

*Pilots refer to newer planes like the Boeing 777 and the Airbus 320 synecdochically as "glass cockpits," planes in which the information most frequently reviewed is displayed in color overlays on videolike screens. The instrument cluster in older jet aircraft is referred to collectively as "steam gauges."

tudes, when ground marks like pipelines and lakes were more important to navigation. Today, in advanced aircraft, they routinely fly high above the weather, on automatic pilot, and descend less often for fuel. A dispatcher in a windowless international office half a world away may organize a sense of geography for them and radio in, even telephone with any changes in the flight plan, due, say, to increased storm activity. There's little need to watch the weather, or anything else.

Pilots say they "fly by wire" now, no longer sensing the plane's response in their hands and feet. They refer to "cockpit management skills" more often than their "stick-and-rudder ability." In the 747-400, they monitor six separate cathode-ray screens, mesmerizing as small televisions. In this kind of self-absorbed travel, built on a dashboard knowledge of one's surroundings, a sense of both geographic scale and particularity is ruptured. Flights cover huge distances in a few hours; matriculation at a chain hotel, often reached on a crew bus driven down an advertising corridor like the airport's passenger corridors, is brief. English is spoken everywhere. Anacin, 7-Up, *Rambo,* CNN, Ray-Ban, and *Time* are omnipresent. Reality outside the plane slowly merges with a comforting, authoritative, and self-referential world found within it.

Jet lag is popularly construed as an affliction of the unseasoned traveler, a preventable distraction. No pilot I talked to regarded it as such but rather as a sort of spatial and temporal abuse which, by the time you reach your fifties, can overwhelm you on a single trip.

Over many days of flying, I fought my own idiosyncratic battle with jet lag, following the common advice of pilots to sleep when you're tired and eat when you're hungry. When I got home, after traveling 30,000 or 40,000 miles in ten days, I would fall into bed like an iron ingot dropped in the dust. On the road, like the pilots, I endured the symptoms of a jagged, asynchronous life. No matter how exhilarating a trip might have been, I sensed upon leaving the plane that a thrashing like the agitation of a washing machine had ended, and that, slightly dazed, I was now drifting off my path, a yawning ship. My tissues felt leaden. Memory seemed a pea suspended in the empty hulk of my body. I had the impression my mind was searching for the matching ends of myriad broken connections and that it was vaguely panicked by the effort. The fabric of awareness felt discontinuous. Time shoaled, losing its familiar depth and resonance. I craved darkness and stillness. I believed that without darkness and stillness no dreams would come and that without dreams there would be no recovery. Once, in a hotel, I slept on solely to dream.

If you drink copious amounts of water, breathe oxygen occasionally while you're aloft, eat very sparingly during the flight, and decline coffee and other diuretics, you can diminish the effects of jet lag. But the pilots and aeromedical officers I spoke with said the symptoms are so inevitable and intractable, you have to learn to accommodate them.

Pilots get regular checkups, many of them exercise, and most appear and feel fit. The physical hazards of long-term flying are relatively minor—an increased incidence of cataracts, high-frequency hearing loss (beginning in the right ear for copilots and becoming more severe in the left

ear with pilots)—or are unknown—the effect, for example, of regular exposure to high doses of cosmic radiation.
Pilots more than copilots will tell you that whatever health
hazards they may face, they love flying too much to give it
up. Many think that jet lag is the principal cause of chronic
moodiness, a prime source of tension in their domestic
relationships. But they view separation and divorce as grim
contemporary realities, and say resignedly that they are
very well paid for what they do.

I liked the pilots I flew with. They have a remarkable
ability to relax for hours in a state of alertness (pilots
describe the job as "hours of boredom punctuated by minutes of terror"). They seem able to monitor an instrument's unwavering reading and run technical checklists
repeatedly without mentally wandering or reimagining the
information. Their hand movements in the cockpit are
slow, smooth, direct; they concentrate on precision and
routine, on thoroughness. The virtues they admire—dedi-
cation to a job, loyalty, allegiance to a code—are more military than corporate. Some, like generals, carry with them
a peculiar, haggard isolation.

Standing between the pilots on the Singapore flight, my
neck bowed beneath the overhead instrument panel, I
could take the most commanding view possible of space
outside the plane. From here, still over the South China
Sea, I could see outlying islands in the Spratly Archipelago
to the southeast. To the northwest were the distant mouths
of the Mekong: Cua Tranh De, Cua Dinh An, Cua Ham
Luong. A while later, Indonesia's Bunguran Selatan Archi-

pelago loomed off the port side, the translucent sea turquoise over its reefs. Afternoon light from the bare orb of the sun filled the clear air at 37,000 feet with a tangible effulgence that made the island of Subi and the water seem closer. We looked down from the keep of our own wind, through layers of wind, to wind on the water; below that, the surface current ran at an angle to currents still deeper. Toward Karimata Strait, between Borneo and Belitung Island to the south, a single layer of thin stratus cloud cast its shadow over a hundred square miles of water. Beyond, the sea was brightly lit once more. Because detail on the water resumed there again with the same brilliance after fading in the foreground, the huge shadow's interruption created the illusion that the distant water was lit by light from another kingdom.

Ending a long silence in the cockpit, the captain said, "The Earth is beautiful."

On our approach to Singapore smoke began pouring out of the window vents—warm, humid air from outside condensing in our dry interior. The pilots enjoyed my alarm.

On the ground, while the plane was unloaded, and then reloaded for Bangkok and Tokyo, I strolled through mown grasses in an adjacent field. Two common mynah birds landed on the plane's port wing.

VI

The hotel in Seoul was just west of Mt. Namsan Park in Yongsan-Ku, in the city's southwest quarter. The crew bus would not leave for the airport for four hours, and I had risen before sunrise to take a long walk. I wanted to see things that couldn't be purchased.

I walked north from the hotel through a cramped residential district. Seoul is a city of granite hills, of crags and pinnacles. On this winter morning it filled gradually with a diffuse gray light under heavy, overcast skies. As I wandered the narrow streets, I endeavored not to seem too curious about what was displayed on the shelves of small stores attached to small two-story houses. Instead I observed what sort of bicycles people rode, what kind of clothing they wore against the cold—indigenous solutions to common problems. I studied the spines of books displayed in a window, the Chinese, Japanese, and Korean titles mixed, their ideograms so clearly different in comparison. I could not see past a street reflection in the window glass whether a companion volume was in Arabic.

Some Westerners traveling today in the Middle East may experience what they take for irritation over religious differences; in Seoul—or Bangkok or Wuhan—the look a Westerner may get walking through residential streets seems more often one of resentment or bewilderment at the imposition of economic change. You are the one responsible, the looks imply, for swift, large-scale painful alterations to my culture; you see them as improvements, but they are designed really only to make business—your sort of business—flow more smoothly. It is you, they seem to say, who define, often and titanically, what is of value.

What I felt—the discomforting gospel of world-encircling consumerism of which I was an inadvertent symbol—I could have felt as an indictment in a dozen other cities. It needn't have been here, where I only wanted relief from the impact of culture I felt every time the plane landed.

Early in the morning in a city like this, you may see several hundred years of history unfold in just a few hours. The earliest people out are those packing fish up from boats on the Han River, people selling charcoal to shopkeepers or transporting food in handcarts, a manner of life relatively unchanged from 1750. Appearing later are factory workers, headed for parts of Seoul where the smoke and grit ash of nineteenth-century Pittsburgh still cling. Then come department store clerks and employees of large firms, the lower and middle levels of white-collar work. Last out on the sidewalks are expensively dressed men, headed for the Samsung Building or for other corporate offices.

Some in the West see in such rearrangements net gains, others net losses. I do not lean strongly either way, though I'm saddened, as a traveler, by the erosion of languages, the diminishment of other systems of aesthetics, and the loss of what might be called a philosophy of hand tools. It is easy to rue the lack of restraint in promoting consumption as a way of life, but we daily accept myriad commercial solutions to our own discontent—the assuagement of new clothing, new investments, new therapies to ease our disaffections. Some who endure such accelerated living (our advertising presumes) find it a relief periodically to sweep everything into the past, making room for less obligating, more promising products or situations.

It is not difficult to disparage the capitulation in such manic living; what is hard is avoiding the impulse to blame, or the instinct to exempt oneself. Getting dressed at the hotel, I had to smile at the labels in my clothing: J. Crew, Gap, Territory Ahead, Patagonia. My shoes, dark brown suede wingtips, had been made in Korea.

Once, suspended over the North Pacific, I held the image of a loom in my mind. If these flights back and forth across the Pacific are the weft, I wondered, what is the warp, the world already strung, through which my shuttle cuts back and forth? And what pattern will the weave produce?

I picked my way around rain-pocked mounds of snow back to the hotel, down tight alleys backed with fishmongers' crates.

The plane I boarded out of Seoul was a passenger flight with lower-deck cargo for Narita. There I boarded a freighter bound for New York via Anchorage. In the Jeppesen Manual that most United States pilots carry—a two-inch-thick ring binder of tissue-thin pages containing detailed information about airports—Anchorage is described as a consistently dangerous place to get in and out of. The nearby area experiences a lot of wind shear and turbulence; icing is common in winter.★

Pilots recall with little prompting the details of commercial airplane crashes going back many years. Each one is a warning. Their interest is almost entirely technical and legal, not macabre. While I was flying in the Middle East a freighter crashed in Kansas City, killing the three pilots

★The turbulence we encountered over Anchorage on the flight with the horses was the worst one pilot had ever experienced. On another flight outbound from Anchorage, the freighter built up the heaviest loads of ice the chief pilot had ever had to contend with.

aboard. Although the crew I was with read the story in the *International Herald Tribune,* no one commented. The pilots presume such reports are always confused and therefore misleading. They wait instead for the National Transportation Safety Board findings to appear in *Aviation Week and Space Technology.*

We had no trouble getting into or out of Anchorage, and we enjoyed an unperturbed flight to New York, with spectacular views of the Canadian Rockies. On the next leg, from JFK to San Francisco, I fell into conversation with the pilot about the history of aerodynamic design that produced the 747. Like many pilots, he had an intuitive sense of the volume of abstract space, and he was a gazer-out-of-windows. It was about one in the morning. Air-traffic control in New York had given us a direct path to San Francisco. Our flight plan showed no areas of turbulence ahead, and no one in front of us was reporting any. The moonless sky was glimmering, deep. I asked the pilot if he had ever heard of James Turrell. He hadn't.

I'd hoped for weeks to speak with someone who had. Turrell is best known for an enormous project called Roden Crater near Flagstaff in northern Arizona. He reconformed the crater with bulldozers and road graders, believing celestial space actually had shape, that one could perceive the "celestial vault" above the Earth, and that a view from within the crater could reveal that architecture by so disposing the viewer. Turell, a pilot, once said, "For me, flying really dealt with these spaces delineated by air conditions, by visual penetration, by sky conditions; some were visual, some were only felt. These are the kinds of space I wanted to work with."

People who have traveled to Roden Crater—heavy-equipment operators as well as museum curators—say, yes, you do see that the sky has shape from the crater. I'd like to go, I told the pilot.

After a while the pilot turned around in his seat and said, "He's right. I know what he's talking about. The space you fly the plane through has shape." I asked if he thought time had boundary or dimension, and told him what I had felt at Cape Town, that time pooled in every part of the world as if in a basin. The dimension, the transparency, and the agitation were everywhere different. He nodded, as if together we were working out an equation.

A while later he said, "Being 'on time' is like being on fire."

One of my last flights takes me to Buenos Aires, seat of the old viceroyalty on the Río de la Plata, the river of silver. Here, as in other places I visited, people in the freight depot are friendly and open, and sometimes quite sophisticated about ironies in the airfreight business. I go to lunch with four men who treat me to a meal of Argentine beef and a good Argentine red wine. Affecting philosophical detachment, they explain the non-European way to conduct business in Buenos Aires, the paths money might take here. We laugh. Three of us then go to a strong room to inspect a shipment of gold bullion.

I walk out to the tarmac afterward with the KLM freight manager. He is directing the loading of Flight 798 from Buenos Aires to Amsterdam, a thirteen-hour run. In the crackle blast of combusting kerosene, swept by hot winds,

I watch the pallets go aboard. These, I have come to understand, are the goods. This lovely, shrieking behemoth, the apotheosis of modern imagination and invention, is being filled yet again with what we believe in. I watch, as agnostics must once have watched at Chartres, for a sign, a confirmation of faith. I see frozen trout; fresh strawberries; eighty cases of live worms; seventy-three pounds of gold for Geneva, packed in light green metal boxes sealed with embossed aluminum bands, wrapped in clear plastic, banded again with steel strapping. An armed security officer stands by until the bulk-cargo door is closed, then stands at a distance, watching.

The last load in the aft compartment is four tons of horsemeat. The temperature is set at 53 degrees and the door is closed. The last load in the forward compartment will be 175 penguins. They have come in on the plane from Santiago and are headed for Tokyo. They wait in the noise and heat around the airplane while freight in the forward compartment is rearranged, the weight more evenly distributed.

The penguins stand erect in narrow cells, five cells forming a wooden crate. A wire mesh panel on the front, beginning at chest level, slants up and back, reaching the top of the crate just above their head height. So constructed, air can reach those on the inside of the load, thirty-five crates stacked in tiers on a single pallet. The gangs of five face in four directions; some see us, some see one another, some see the plane, some the back of another box. I recognize magellanic and rockhopper penguins. If they're making any noise I cannot hear it over the jet engines. A few strike at the wire mesh with their bills. Some of the rockhoppers rise on their toes, cramping their heads, and flap their flippers repeatedly against the dividers.

After they are loaded, the temperature of their compartment is set at 43 degrees and the door is closed.

KL 798, a passenger flight, takes us up the southern coast of Brazil, above the Serra do Mar and Serra do Espinhaço and out over the Atlantic near Natal. There is a lightning storm near Recife, on the coast. I send my worn letter of introduction to the cockpit to see if it would be possible to watch and talk for a while. The purser comes back with a smile. Yes.

I take my place in the jump seat, assure the chief pilot I am familiar with how to operate the oxygen mask and with my responsibilities in case of an emergency. This is a 747-400. With this new design, the flight engineer's job has been eliminated; a relief crew of two is now asleep in bunks along the port side, just aft of the cockpit.

We watch cobra strikes of yellow-and-blue light on the starboard horizon. Against the display of lightning I hesitate to speak. I take in the instruments to learn our heading, the speed and direction of the wind, our altitude, the outside temperature. I'm aware of my faith in the integrity of the aircraft. I recognize the familiar, impetuous hurtling toward the void, a space to be filled only briefly, then to yawn again, hopeful and acquisitive.

Out over the Atlantic I lean forward and ask the captain how long he's been flying, which routes he knows best. Twenty-eight years, he says. He speaks of the South American and Caribbean routes. I think of the penguins two decks below, whose wings have become flippers, slamming them against the walls of their pens.

THE AMERICAN GEOGRAPHIES

It has become commonplace to observe that Americans know little of the geography of their country, that they are innocent of it as a landscape of rivers, mountains, and towns. They do not know, supposedly, the location of the Delaware Water Gap, the Olympic Mountains, or the Piedmont Plateau; and, the indictment continues, they have little conception of the way the individual components of this landscape are imperiled, from a human perspective, by modern farming practices or industrial pollution.

I do not know how true this is, but it is easy to believe that it is truer than most of us would wish. A recent Gallup Organization and National Geographic Society survey found Americans woefully ignorant of world geography. Three out of four couldn't locate the Persian Gulf. The implication was that we knew no more about our own homeland, and that this ignorance undermined the integrity of our political processes and the efficiency of our business enterprises.

As Americans, we profess a sincere and fierce love for the

American landscape, for our rolling prairies, free-flowing rivers, and "purple mountains' majesty"; but it is hard to imagine, actually, where this particular landscape is. It is not just that a nostalgic landscape has passed away—Mark Twain's Mississippi is now dammed from Illinois to Louisiana and the prairies have all been sold and fenced. It is that it's always been a romantic's landscape. In the attenuated form in which it is presented on television today, in magazine articles and in calendar photographs, the essential wildness of the American landscape is reduced to attractive scenery. We look out on a familiar, memorized landscape that portends adventure and promises enrichment. There are no distracting people in it and few artifacts of human life. The animals are all beautiful, diligent, one might even say well behaved. Nature's unruliness, the power of rivers and skies to intimidate, and any evidence of disastrous human land management practices are all but invisible. It is, in short, a magnificent garden, a colonial vision of paradise imposed on a real place that is, at best, only selectively known.

The real American landscape is a face of almost incomprehensible depth and complexity. If one were to sit for a few days, for example, among the ponderosa pine forests and black lava fields of the Cascade Mountains in western Oregon, inhaling the pines' sweet balm on an evening breeze from some point on the barren rock, and then were to step off to the Olympic Peninsula in Washington, to those rain forests with sphagnum moss floors soft as fleece underfoot and Douglas firs too big around for five people to hug, and then head south to walk the ephemeral creeks and sun-blistered playas of the Mojave Desert in southern California, one would be reeling under the sensations. The contrast is not only one of plants and soils, a different array, say, of brilliantly colored beetles. The shock to the senses comes from a different shape to the silence, a difference in the very quality of light, in the weight of the air. And this relatively short journey down the West Coast would still leave the traveler with all that lay to the east to explore— the anomalous sand hills of Nebraska, the heat and frog voices of Okefenokee Swamp, the fetch of Chesapeake Bay, the hardwood copses and black bears of the Ozark Mountains.

No one of these places, of course, can be entirely fathomed, biologically or aesthetically. They are mysteries upon which we impose names. Enchantments. We tick the names off glibly but lovingly. We mean no disrespect. Our genuine desire, though we may be skeptical about the time it would take and uncertain of its practical value to us, is to actually know these places. As deeply ingrained in the American psyche as the desire to conquer and control the land is the desire to sojourn in it, to sail up and down Pamlico Sound, to paddle a canoe through Minnesota's boundary waters, to walk on the desert of the Great Salt Lake, to camp in the stony hardwood valleys of Vermont.

To do this well, to really come to an understanding of a specific American geography, requires not only time but a kind of local expertise, an intimacy with place few of us ever develop. There is no way around the former requirement: if you want to know you must take the time. It is not in books. A specific geographical understanding, however, can be sought out and borrowed. It resides with men and women more or less sworn to a place, who abide there, who have a feel for the soil and history, for the turn of leaves and night sounds. Often they are glad to take the outlander in tow.

These local geniuses of American landscape, in my experience, are people in whom geography thrives. They are the antithesis of geographical ignorance. Rarely known outside their own communities, they often seem, at the first encounter, unremarkable and anonymous. They may not be able to recall the name of a particular wildflower— or they may have given it a name known only to them. They might have forgotten the precise circumstances of a local historical event. Or they can't say for certain when the last of the Canada geese passed through in the fall, or can't differentiate between two kinds of trout in the same creek. Like all of us, they have fallen prey to the fallacies of memory and are burdened with ignorance; but they are nearly flawless in the respect they bear these places they love. Their knowledge is intimate rather than encyclopedic, human but not necessarily scholarly. It rings with the concrete details of experience.

America, I believe, teems with such people. The paradox here, between a faulty grasp of geographical knowledge for which Americans are indicted and the intimate, apparently contradictory familiarity of a group of largely anonymous people, is not solely a matter of confused scale. (The local landscape is easier to know than a national landscape—and many local geographers, of course, are relatively ignorant of a national geography.)

And it is not simply ironic. The paradox is dark. To be succinct: the politics and advertising that seek a national audience must project a national geography; to be broadly useful that geography must, inevitably, be generalized and it is often romantic. It is therefore frequently misleading and imprecise. The same holds true with the entertainment industry, but here the problem might be clearer. The same films, magazines, and television features that honor an imaginary American landscape also tout the worth of the anonymous men and women who interpret it. Their affinity for the land is lauded, their local allegiance admired. But the rigor of their local geographies, taken as a whole, contradicts a patriotic, national vision of unspoiled, untroubled land. These men and women are ultimately forgotten, along with the details of the landscapes they speak for, in the face of more pressing national matters. It is the chilling nature of modern society to find an ignorance of geography, local or national, as excusable as an ignorance of hand tools; and to find the commitment of people to their home places only momentarily entertaining. And finally naïve.

If one were to pass time among Basawara people in the Kalahari Desert, or with Tikuna on the upper Amazon, or with Pitjantjatjara Aborigines in Australia, the most salient impression they might leave is of an absolutely stunning knowledge of their local geography—geology, hydrology, biology, and weather. In short, the extensive particulars of their intercourse with it.

In forty thousand years of human history, it has only been in the last few hundred years or so that a people could afford to ignore their local geographies as completely as we do and still survive. Technological innovations from refrigerated trucks to artificial fertilizers, from sophisticated cost accounting to mass air transportation, have utterly changed concepts of season, distance, soil productivity, and the real cost of drawing sustenance from the land. It is now possible for a resident of Kansas City to bite into a fresh mango in the dead of winter; for someone in San Francisco to travel to Atlanta in a few hours with no worry of how formidable might be crossings of the Great Basin Desert or the Mississippi River; for an absentee farmer to gain a tax advantage from a farm that leaches poisons into its water table and on which crops are left to rot. The Pitjantjatjara might shake their heads in bewilderment and bemusement, not because they are primitive or ignorant people, not because they have no sense of irony or are incapable of marveling, but because they have not (many would say not yet) realized a world in which such manipulation of the land—surmounting the imperatives of distance it imposes, for example, or turning the large-scale destruction of forests and arable land into wealth—is desirable or plausible.

In the years I have traveled through America, in cars and on horseback, on foot and by raft, I have repeatedly been brought to a sudden state of awe by some gracile or savage movement of animal, some odd wrapping of a tree's foliage by the wind, an unimpeded run of dew-laden prairie stretching to a horizon flat as a coin where a pin-dot sun pales the dawn sky pink. I know these things are beyond intellection, that they are the vivid edges of a world that includes but also transcends the human world. In memory, when I dwell on these things, I know that in a truly national literature there should be odes to the Triassic reds of the Colorado Plateau, to the sharp and ghostly light of the Florida

Keys, to the aeolian soils of southern Minnesota and the Palouse in Washington, though the modern mind abjures the literary potential of such subjects. (If the sand and floodwater farmers of Arizona and New Mexico were to take the black loams of Louisiana in their hands they would be flabbergasted, and that is the beginning of literature.) I know there should be eloquent evocations of the cobbled beaches of Maine, the plutonic walls of the Sierra Nevada, the orange canyons of the Kaibab Plateau. I have no doubt, in fact, that there are. They are as numerous and diverse as the eyes and fingers that ponder the country—it is that only a handful of them are known. The great majority are to be found in drawers and boxes, in the letters and private journals of millions of workaday people who have regarded their encounters with the land as an engagement bordering on the spiritual, as being fundamentally linked to their state of health.

One cannot acknowledge the extent and the history of this kind of testimony without being forced to the realization that something strange, if not dangerous, is afoot. Year by year, the number of people with firsthand experience in the land dwindles. Rural populations continue to shift to the cities. The family farm is in a state of demise, and government and industry continue to apply pressure on the native peoples of North America to sever their ties with the land. In the wake of this loss of personal and local knowledge, the knowledge from which a real geography is derived, the knowledge on which a country must ultimately stand, has come something hard to define but I think sinister and unsettling—the packaging and marketing of land as a form of entertainment. An incipient industry,

capitalizing on the nostalgia Americans feel for the imagined virgin landscapes of their ancestors, and on a desire for
adventure, now offers people a convenient though sometimes incomplete or even spurious geography as an induce-
ment to purchase a unique experience. But the line between
authentic experience and a superficial exposure to the elements of experience is blurred. And the real landscape, in
all its complexity, is distorted even further in the public
imagination. No longer innately mysterious and dignified,
a ground from which experience grows, it becomes a curi-
ously generic backdrop on which experience is imposed.

In theme parks the profound, subtle, and protracted
experience of running a river is reduced to a loud, quick,
safe equivalence, a pleasant distraction. People only able to
venture into the countryside on annual vacations are,
increasingly, schooled in the belief that wild land will, and
should, provide thrills and exceptional scenery on a timely
basis. If it does not, something is wrong, either with the
land itself or possibly with the company outfitting the trip.

People in America, then, face a convoluted situation.
The land itself, vast and differentiated, defies the notion of
a national geography. If applied at all it must be applied
lightly, and it must grow out of the concrete detail of local
geographies. Yet Americans are daily presented with, and
have become accustomed to talking about, a homogenized
national geography, one that seems to operate indepen-
dently of the land, a collection of objects rather than a
continuous bolt of fabric. It appears in advertisements, as a
background in movies, and in patriotic calendars. The suggestion is that there *can* be a national geography because
the constituent parts are interchangeable and can be treated

as commodities. In day-to-day affairs, in other words, one place serves as well as another to convey one's point. On reflection, this is an appalling condescension and a terrible imprecision, the very antithesis of knowledge. The idea that either the Green River in Utah or the Salmon River in Idaho will do, or that the valleys of Kentucky and West Virginia are virtually interchangeable, is not just misleading. For people still dependent on the soil for their sustenance, or for people whose memories tie them to those places, it betrays a numbing casualness, a utilitarian, expedient, and commercial frame of mind. It heralds a society in which it is no longer necessary for human beings to know where they live, except as those places are described and fixed by numbers. The truly difficult and lifelong task of discovering where one lives is finally disdained.

If a society forgets or no longer cares where it lives, then anyone with the political power and the will to do so can manipulate the landscape to conform to certain social ideals or nostalgic visions. People may hardly notice that anything has happened, or assume that whatever happens—a mountain stripped of timber and eroding into its creeks—is for the common good. The more superficial a society's knowledge of the real dimensions of the land it occupies becomes, the more vulnerable the land is to exploitation, to manipulation for short-term gain. The land, virtually powerless before political and commercial entities, finds itself finally with no defenders. It finds itself bereft of intimates with indispensable, concrete knowledge. (Oddly, or perhaps not oddly, while American society continues to value local knowledge as a quaint part of its heritage, it continues to cut such people off from any real political power. This is as true for small farmers and illiterate cowboys as it is for American Indians, native Hawaiians, and Eskimos.)

The intense pressure of imagery in America, and the manipulation of images necessary to a society with specific goals, means the land will inevitably be treated like a commodity; and voices that tend to contradict the proffered image will, one way or another, be silenced or discredited by those in power. This is not new to America; the promulgation in America of a false or imposed geography has been the case from the beginning. All local geographies, as they were defined by hundreds of separate, independent native traditions, were denied in the beginning in favor of an imported and unifying vision of America's natural history. The country, the landscape itself, was eventually defined according to dictates of Progress like Manifest Destiny, and laws like the Homestead Act which reflected a poor understanding of the physical lay of the land.

When I was growing up in southern California, I formed the rudiments of a local geography—eucalyptus trees, February rains, desert cottontails. I lost much of it when my family moved to New York City, a move typical of the modern, peripatetic style of American life, responding to the exigencies of divorce and employment. As a boy I felt a hunger to know the American landscape that was extreme; when I was finally able to travel on my own, I did so. Eventually I visited most of the United States, living for brief periods of time in Arizona, Indiana, Alabama, Georgia, Wyoming, New Jersey, and Montana before settling years ago in western Oregon.

The astonishing level of my ignorance confronted me everywhere I went. I knew early on that the country could not be held together in a few phrases, that its geography was magnificent and incomprehensible, that a man or woman could devote a lifetime to its elucidation and still feel in the end that he or she had but sailed many thousands of miles over the surface of the ocean. So I came into the habit of traversing landscapes I wanted to know with local tutors and reading what had previously been written about, and in, those places. I came to value exceedingly novels and essays and works of nonfiction that connected human enterprise to real and specific places, and I grew to be mildly distrustful of work that occurred in no particular place, work so cerebral and detached as to be refutable only in an argument of ideas.

These sojourns in various corners of the country infused me, somewhat to my surprise on thinking about it, with a great sense of hope. Whatever despair I had come to feel at a waning sense of the real land and the emergence of false geographies—elements of the land being manipulated, for example, to create erroneous but useful patterns in advertising—was dispelled by the depth of a single person's local knowledge, by the serenity that seemed to come with that intelligence. Any harm that might be done by people who cared nothing for the land, to whom it was not innately worthy but only something ultimately for sale, I thought, would one day have to meet this kind of integrity, people with the same dignity and transcendence as the land they occupied. So when I traveled, when I rolled my sleeping bag out on the shores of the Beaufort Sea or in the high pastures of the Absaroka Range in Wyoming, or at the bottom of the Grand Canyon, I absorbed those particular testaments to life, the indigenous color and songbird song, the smell of sun-bleached rock, damp earth, and wild honey, with some crude appreciation of the singular magnificence of each of those places. And the reassurance I felt expanded in the knowledge that there were, and would likely always be, people speaking out whenever they felt the dignity of the earth imperiled in these places.

The promulgation of false geographies, which threaten the fundamental notion of what it means to live somewhere, is a current with a stable and perhaps growing countercurrent. People living in New York City are familiar with the stone basements, the cratonic geology, of that island and have a feeling for birds migrating through in the fall, their sequence and number. They do not find the city alien but human, its attenuated natural history merely different from that of rural Georgia or Wisconsin. I find the countermeasure, too, among Eskimos who cannot read but who might engage you for days on the subtleties of sea-ice topography. And among men and women who, though they have followed in the footsteps of their parents, have come to the conclusion that they cannot farm or fish or log in the way their ancestors did; the finite boundaries to this sort of wealth have appeared in their lifetime. Or among young men and women who have taken several decades of book-learned agronomy, zoology, silviculture and horticulture, ecology, ethnobotany, and fluvial geomorphology and turned it into a new kind of local knowledge, who have taken up residence in a place and sought, both because of and in spite of their education, to develop a deep intimacy with it. Or they have gone to work, idealistically, for the National Park Service or the fish and wildlife services or for a private institution like the Nature Conservancy. They are people to whom the land is more than politics or economics. These are people for whom the land is alive. It feeds them, directly, and that is how and why they learn its geography.

In the end, then, if you begin among the blue crabs of Chesapeake Bay and wander for several years, down through the Smoky Mountains and back to the bluegrass hills, along the drainages of the Ohio and into the hill country of Missouri, where in summer a chorus of cicadas might drown out human conversation, then up the Missouri itself, reading on the way the entries of Meriwether Lewis and William Clark and musing on the demise of the plains grizzly and the sturgeon, cross west into the drainage of the Platte and spend the evenings with Gene Weltfish's *The Lost Universe,* her book about the Pawnee who once thrived there, then drop south to Palo Duro Canyon and the irrigated farms of the Llano Estacado in Texas, turn west across the Sangre de Cristo, southernmost of the Rocky Mountain ranges, and move north and west up onto the slickrock mesas of Utah, those browns and oranges, the ocherous hues reverberating in the deep canyons, then go north, swinging west to the insular ranges that sit like battleships in the pelagic space of Nevada, camp at the steaming edge of sulphur springs in the Black Rock Desert, where alkaline pans are glazed with a ferocious light, a heat to melt iron, then cross the northern Sierra Nevada, waist-deep in summer snow in the passes, to descend to the valley of the Sacramento, and rise through groves of elephantine redwoods in the Coast Range, to arrive at Cape Mendocino, before Balboa's Pacific, cormorants and gulls, gray whales headed north for Unimak Pass in the Aleutians, the winds crashing down on you, facing the ocean over the blue ocean that gives the scene its true vastness, making this crossing, having been so often astonished at the line and the color of the land, the ingenious lives of its plants and animals, the varieties of its darknesses, the intensity of the stars overhead, you would be ashamed to discover, then, in yourself, any capacity to focus on ravages in the land that left you unsettled. You would have seen so much, breathtaking, startling, and outsize, that you might not be able for a long time to break the spell, the sense, especially finishing your journey in the West, that the land had not been as rearranged or quite as compromised as you had first imagined.

After you had slept some nights on the beach, however, with that finite line of the ocean before you and the land stretching out behind you, the wind first battering then cradling you, you would be compelled by memory, obligated by your own involvement, to speak of what left you troubled. To find the rivers dammed and shrunken, the soil washed away, the land fenced, a tracery of pipes and wires and roads laid down everywhere, blocking and channeling the movement of water and animals, cutting the eye off repeatedly and confining it—you had expected this. It troubles you no more than your despair over the ruthlessness, the insensitivity, the impetuousness of modern life. What underlies this obvious change, however, is a less noticeable pattern of disruption: acidic lakes, skies empty of birds, fouled beaches, the poisonous slags of industry, the sun burning like a molten coin in ruined air.

It is a tenet of certain ideologies that man is responsible for all that is ugly, that everything nature creates is beautiful. Nature's darkness goes partly unreported, of course, and human brilliance is often perversely ignored. What is true is that man has a power, literally beyond his comprehension, to destroy. The lethality of some of what he manufactures, the incompetence with which he stores it or seeks to dispose of it, the cavalier way in which he employs in his daily living substances that threaten his health, the leniency of the courts in these matters (as though products as well as people enjoyed the protection of the Fifth Amendment), and the treatment of open land, rivers, and the atmosphere as if, in some medieval way, they could still be regarded as disposal sinks of infinite capacity, would make you wonder, standing face to in the wind at Cape Mendocino, if we weren't bent on an errand of madness.

The geographies of North America, the myriad small landscapes that make up the national fabric, are threatened—by ignorance of what makes them unique, by utilitarian attitudes, by failure to include them in the moral universe, and by brutal disregard. A testament of minor voices can clear away an ignorance of any place, can inform us of its special qualities; but no voice, by merely telling a story, can cause the poisonous wastes that saturate some parts of the land to decompose, to evaporate. This responsibility falls ultimately to the national community, a vague and fragile entity to be sure, but one that, in America, can be ferocious in exerting its will.

Geography, the formal way in which we grapple with this areal mystery, is finally knowledge that calls up something in the land we recognize and respond to. It gives us a sense of place and a sense of community. Both are indispensable to a state of well-being, an individual's and a country's.

One afternoon on the Siuslaw River in the Coast Range of Oregon, in January, I hooked a steelhead, a sea-run trout, that told me, through the muscles of my hands and arms and shoulders, something of the nature of the thing I was calling "the Siuslaw River." Years ago I had stood under a pecan tree in Upson County, Georgia, idly eating the nuts, when slowly it occurred to me that these nuts would taste different from pecans growing somewhere up in South Carolina. I didn't need a sharp sense of taste to know this, only to pay attention at a level no one had ever told me was necessary. One November dawn, long before the sun rose, I began a vigil at the Dumont Dunes in the Mojave Desert in California, which I kept until a few minutes after the sun broke the horizon. During that time I named to myself the colors by which the sky changed and by which the sand itself flowed like a rising tide through grays and silvers and blues into yellows, pinks, washed duns, and fallow beiges.

It is through the power of observation, the gifts of eye and ear, of tongue and nose and finger, that a place first rises up in our mind; afterward it is memory that carries the place, that allows it to grow in depth and complexity. For as long as our records go back, we have held these two things dear, landscape and memory. Each infuses us with a different kind of life. The one feeds us, figuratively and literally. The other protects us from lies and tyranny. To keep landscapes intact and the memory of them, our history in them, alive, seems as imperative a task in modern time as finding the extent to which individual expression can be accommodated before it threatens to destroy the fabric of society.

If I were to now visit another country, I would ask my local companion, before I saw any museum or library, any factory or fabled town, to walk me in the country of his or her youth, to tell me the names of things and how, traditionally, they have been fitted together in a community. I would ask for the stories, the voice of memory over the land. I would ask to taste the wild nuts and fruits, to see their fishing lures, their bouquets, their fences. I would ask about the history of storms there, the age of the trees, the winter color of the hills. Only then would I ask to see the museums. I would want first the sense of a real place, to know that I was not inhabiting an idea. I would want to know the lay of the land first, the real geography, and take some measure of the love of it in my companion before I stood before the paintings or read works of scholarship. I would want to have something real and remembered against which I might hope to measure their truth.

from ARCTIC DREAMS

On a warm summer day in 1823, the *Cumbrian,* a 360-ton British whaler, sailed into the waters off Pond's Bay (now Pond Inlet), northern Baffin Island, after a short excursion to the north. The waters of Lancaster Sound, where she had been, were supposed to be a promising "new water," but the *Cumbrian* hadn't struck a whale in two weeks of cruising. Worse, in her captain's view, the forty-odd ships that had chosen instead to dally at the mouth of Pond's Bay had met with spectacular success in her absence. "Several ships," lamented Captain Johnson in his log, "had captured upwards of 12, one or two [ships] 15 apiece, and one had got full. . . ."

But the *Cumbrian* did not have long to wait. The newly discovered waters of western Baffin Bay, the West Water, teemed with the men's special prey, the Greenland whale. On the very next day, July 28, they killed three. In the days that followed they took another twelve, for a total of twenty-three for the season. On August 20 the *Cumbrian* sailed for ice-free waters off the coast of Greenland and then doubled Cape Farewell for England. The whale blubber she carried would render 236 tons of oil to light the street lamps of Great Britain and process the coarse wool of its textile mills. Also in her hold were more than four and a half tons of whalebone (baleen), to be turned into umbrella staves and venetian blinds, portable sheep pens, window gratings, and furniture springing.

The *Cumbrian* made port at Hull on September 26, to dockside cheers. Young boys from town swarmed her rigging in quest of the traditional garland of sun-bleached ribbons, halfway up the main-topgallant mast. The ship's owners beamed with pleasure. The year before the *Cumbrian* had taken but half this many whales, for no ship that year had been able to breach the ice in Davis Strait. And in 1821 the *Cumbrian* had returned with grim news—three ships from Hull, and at least four others from British ports, were lost, crushed in the ice.

The season of 1823 eased these awful memories. The West Water off Pond's Bay seemed most promising. And the *Cumbrian* had also brought back walrus hides and ivory, traded from the Eskimos of West Greenland and northern Baffin Island. And also several narwhal tusks. If the prices for oil and whalebone held, if there were a few good ice-years back to back, and if London didn't rescind the industry's price supports or abolish the protective trade tariffs . . .

None of this had been much on the minds of the men of the *Cumbrian*. In the West Water, they had worked the odd hours of men who knew no night, who jumped for the whaleboat davits whenever a "fish" was sighted. They slept sprawled on the decks and ate irregularly. Their days in the ice were heady, the weather splendid. The distant landscapes of Bylot and Baffin islands at Pond's Bay were etched brilliantly before them by a high-tempered light in air clear as gin—an unearthly sight that filled them with a mixture of disbelief and pleasure. They felt exhilaration in the constant light; and a sense of satisfaction and worth, which came partly from their arduous work.

The summer of 1823 marked a high point in the halcyon days of British arctic whaling, which followed the close of the Napoleonic Wars. The discovery of the West Water came at a time when the market for whale products was resurgent, and it made the merchants and investors of Hull and Peterhead, of Dundee and Aberdeen and Whitby, a rich bounty between 1818 and 1824. In 1825 it would begin to unravel—technological advances and British economic policy would weaken the home and foreign markets for oil and whalebone, and the too-frequent and expensive loss of uninsured ships would dry up investment capital. With 2000 whales killed in 1823 alone, overfishing, too, would begin to be a problem.

The object of all this attention was a creature the British had been hunting commercially for 212 years, first in the bays of Spitsbergen and in the loose pack ice of the Greenland Sea, then in the southern reaches of Davis Strait, and finally in the North Water and West Water of Baffin Bay. Long slats of blue-black, plankton-straining baleen hung from the roof of its mouth in a U-shaped curtain, some of the blades nearly 15 feet long. The stout body, with a massive head one-third the animal's length, was wrapped in blubber as much as 20 inches thick—a higher ratio of blubber to weight than that for any other whale. The blubber of a good-size animal might yield 25 tons of oil; its 300 or more baleen plates might mean more than a ton of whalebone. The 45-foot carcass—minus baleen and its flukes (taken to make glue) and flensed of its blubber—was cut adrift as a "crang" underneath ever-present, mobbing clouds of seabirds.

Because it was a slow swimmer, because it floated when it was killed, and because of the unusual quantity of bone and oil it yielded, it was the right whale to take—the Greenland right. The polar whale. *The* whale. Later, in the western Arctic, it would be called "bowhead," after the outline of its jaw.

The skin of this animal is slightly furrowed to the touch, like coarse-laid paper, and is a velvet-black color softened by gray. Under the chin and on the belly the skin turns white. Its dark brown eyes, the size of an ox's, are nearly lost in the huge head. Its blowhole rises prominently, with the shape of a volcano, allowing the whale to surface in narrow cracks in the sea ice to breathe. It is so sensitive to touch that at a bird's footfall a whale asleep at the surface will start wildly. The fiery pain of a harpoon strike can hardly be imagined. (In 1856 a harpooner aboard the *True-love* reported striking a whale that dived so furiously it took out 1200 yards of line in three and a half minutes before crashing into the ocean floor, breaking its neck and burying its head eight feet deep in blue-black mud.)

Its strength is prodigious. A bowhead harpooned in the Greenland Sea took out 10,440 yards (7000 pounds) of line, snapping two 2¼-inch hemp lines (one of 1560 yards, the other 3360 yards) and pulling an entangled 28-foot whaleboat down with it before it was subdued. On May

27, 1817, thirty hours after it had been harpooned, another Greenland right whale was still towing a fully rigged ship at two knots into a "moderate brisk breeze."

The pursuit of this animal was without restraint. A month before she entered Lancaster Sound in 1823, the *Cumbrian* killed a huge Greenland right, a 57-foot female, in Davis Strait. They came upon her while she was asleep in light ice. Awakened by their approach, she swam slowly once around the ship and then put her head calmly to its bow and began to push. She pushed the ship backward for two minutes before the transfixed crew reacted with harpoons. The incident left the men unsettled. They flinched against such occasional eeriness in their work.

Precisely where they then stood in Davis Strait, off the northern west coast of Greenland, an odd whistling sound was sometimes heard by whalers in calm weather like this—a high note that eventually faded away to a very low note. It was the sign of a gale coming, from the direction most feared in that quarter, the southwest. The louder the whistle, the harder the winds would blow. They heard no whistling that year as they worked their way through the ice streams—but they had not liked the whale pushing against them, as though urging them to go back.

Many were ill at ease with arctic whaling, because of the threat to their lives presented by the unpredictable sea ice; but also in the regions where they hunted they found a beauty more penetrating and sublime than any they had ever known—so they said in their journals. Glaciers collapsed into the dark green sea before them like cliffs of marble as high as the Cliffs of Dover. Winds tore water from melt ponds atop icebergs, to trail off in sheets of rainbowing mists. Pods of white belukha whales glided ghostlike beneath their keels. A thousand auklets roared through the ship's rigging in a wildshower of sound. Walruses with their gleaming tusks and luminous whiskers swam slowly across calm bays in water burning like manganese in the evening sun. Men wrote in earnest, humble prose that they were overwhelmed by the "loveliness and grandeur."

What they saw made the killing seem inappropriate; but it was work, too, security for their families, and they could quickly put compassion and regret aside. "The object of the adventure," wrote one captain, "the value of the prize, the joy of the capture, cannot be sacrificed to feelings of compassion."

On the 27th of July, still lamenting the wasted days cruising in Lancaster Sound, the *Cumbrian* was bearing south along landfast ice east of Bylot Island, past the gruesome evidence of other ships' successes. "Here and there," the log reads, "along the floe edge lay the dead bodies of hundreds of flenched whales . . . the air for miles around was tainted with the foetor which arose from such masses of putridity. Towards evening, the numbers come across were ever increasing, and the effluvia which then assailed our olfactories became almost intolerable."

The northern fulmars and glaucous gulls wheeled and screeched over the crangs. It was the carnage of wealth.

At the southeast tip of Bylot Island that year the local Eskimo, the Tununirmiut, had established a narwhal hunting camp. They traded informally with the British whalers, whom they called *upirnaagiit,* "the men of springtime"—

offering polar bear skins, walrus hides and ivory, and seal-
skin mitts for tin pots, needles, steel knives, and other useful or decorative items. In later years this trading would
become a hedge for shipowners, a commercial necessity
when the whaling alone no longer paid. Ships' captains
would turn to furs, hides, ivory, and the collection of zoo
animals to make ends meet. But those years, years of
exploitation and social change for the Eskimo, lay ahead.
For the moment the Tununirmiut were still aboriginal
hunters, their habits largely unchanged by an availability of
trade goods. They moved nomadically over the sea ice and
the land, according to the itineraries of the animals they
pursued for food, clothing, tools, and utensils.

If one were to generalize about this early trading relationship, it would be to say that the Eskimo were trying to
accommodate themselves—in carefully limited ways—to
an unfamiliar culture that could produce whale meat with
ease, in astonishing quantities in little time, and that also
made available a number of extremely useful items, such as
canvas and saws. The Europeans, looking largely to their
own ends, enjoyed the primitive and exotic aspects of
these encounters. They were eager for souvenirs and sexual
contact with the women, and hoped to trade for a profit.
On those salubrious summer afternoons off Pond's Bay,
then, young native women returned from the whaling
ships to tell their husbands that the white men lived in tiers
of hammocks like *appaliarsuit*—dovekies on a sea cliff. The
husband wiped seal grease from his fingers with a ptarmi-
gan wing and waited to see if she had brought, perhaps,
some tobacco. The Eskimo put a great value on the basic

fact of their own long survival. They were not nearly as taken with the men and their ships as Europeans liked to believe.

The sophistication the whalers felt next to the Eskimo was a false sophistication, and presumptuous. The European didn't value the Eskimo's grasp of the world. And, however clever Eskimos might be with ivory implements and waterproof garments, he thought their techniques dated or simply quaint next to his own. A ship's officer of the time wrote summarily that the Eskimo was "dwindled in his form, his intellect, and his passions." They were people to be taken mild but harmless advantage of, to be chastised like children, but not to be taken seriously. The Europeans called them yaks.

As for the Eskimo, they thought the whalers strange for trying to get on without the skills and companionship of women. They gave them full credit for producing "valuable and convenient articles and implements," but laughed at their inability to clothe, feed, and protect themselves. They regarded the whalers with a mixture of *ilira* and *kappia,* the same emotions a visitor to the modern village of Pond Inlet encounters today. *Ilira* is the fear that accompanies awe; *kappia* is fear in the face of unpredictable violence. Watching a polar bear—*ilira*. Having to cross thin sea ice—*kappia*.

By the summer of 1832, after only a few years of commerce in the region, the whalers were already beginning to find the silent villages of spring—places where everyone had died during the winter of European diphtheria and smallpox. The apparently timeless Arctic, they saw, was in fact changeable. And the vast and particular knowledge of the Eskimo, garnered from hundreds of years of their patient interrogation of the landscape, was starting to slip away.

Far to the northeast of Pond's Bay, west of Cape York on the Greenland coast, was a remarkable phenomenon whalers at the time called the Crimson Cliffs, red-tinged snow they variously explained as due to fungal growth or to the red mute of guillemots feeding on shrimp.★ At an unknown spot to the east of those cliffs, a place the local Eskimos called Savissivik, was a collection of meteorites that the British heard about for the first time in 1818. (The Polar Eskimo chipped bits of iron-nickel from them for harpoon tips and knife blades, and for use in trade with other Eskimos. Among them *savik* meant both "knife" and "iron.") In 1823 even officers of the British whaling fleet had little idea where a meteorite might come from. They couldn't say, either, whether Greenland was actually an island. Nor at that time had anyone been within 500 miles of the North Pole. For all they knew, it was what Henry Hudson believed it was when he sailed for it in 1607, a massive boulder of black basalt sitting in the middle of a warm, calm sea. They were unaware that the Greenland right actually "sang," like the humpback whales they heard in the North Atlantic en route to the arctic fishery. The life history of the Greenland shark, an "unwholesome and lethargic brute" upon which the Danes would build

---

★The tint is from blood-red pigments in the cell walls of species of freshwater algae present on the snow.

Greenland's first commercial fishery (for the oil from its liver), was unknown to them. The existence of a culture that had preceded the Eskimo's in the Arctic was unsuspected, though they traded, unawares, for its artifacts.

In 1823 the North American Arctic was still as distant as fable, inhabited by remarkable animals and uncontacted peoples, the last undiscovered complex ecosystem on the planet. A landscape of numinous events, of a forgiving benediction of light, and a darkness so dunning it precipitated madness; of a cold that froze vinegar, that fractured whatever it penetrated, including the stones. It was uncharted, unclaimed territory, and Europeans had perished miserably in it since the time of the Norse—gangrenous with frostbite, poisoned by polar bear liver, rotted by scurvy, dead of exposure on the ice beside the wreckage of a ship burned to the water line for the last bit of its warmth.

The confidence and élan of the whalemen at Pond's Bay was tempered with this macabre knowledge; and they suspected that their own ignorance of the place, even the ignorance of those among them who made such erudite notes about the biology of whales or the colors of plankton in the current, was extensive. They were overcome, however, by neither fear nor ignorance. Their vessels, for the moment, were "safe as a life boat and tight as a bottle." In two months they would be home to their families, with a year's pay and perhaps a pair of polar bear trousers to show, or a flint-blade knife for a son. And with stories to hold a neighbor enthralled, stories of a breathtaking escape from drowning, or of having collected 6000 eider eggs on a coastal flat one morning. Or of sleeping with an Eskimo woman.

It is easy to imagine their sense of wild adventure, that on one of those July afternoons off Pond's Bay, on a Sunday when a strict Christian captain would permit no whaling, that the crew might be lounging on the sunlit decks comparing exotic arctic souvenirs: the perplexing skull of a muskox, with its massive horn bosses and protruding eye orbitals—"from a kind of polar cattle," as they understood it from the Eskimo, which lived way off to the west and the north. Or a bit of chain mail, which, someone argued, was certain proof that Viking explorers had sailed far north of the Greenland settlements, hundreds of years before. Or a small ivory carving of a human face, twisted in psychotic anguish, an artifact from the vanished Dorset culture. They likely felt a tension between the unfamiliar quality of these objects and the commonplaces of their own daily lives— the boot-worn deck on which they sat, or the intricate but familiar rigging of sails and spars overhead.

Perhaps someone recalled having seen a polar bear once, far offshore in a storm, swimming with measured strokes through great dark seas—and, with that, introduced yet another tension peculiar to the place, that between beauty and violence. Or perhaps they spoke of the Eskimos, how astonishing they were to be able to survive here, how energetic and friendly; and yet how unnerving with their primitive habits: a mother wiping away a child's feces with her hair, a man pinching the heart of a snared bird to kill it, so as not to ruin the feathers.

In their own separate, spare quarters, the ship's officers might have been reading William Scoresby's *Account of the Arctic Regions* or the recently published discovery narrative of William Parry, who had opened the way to the West

Water in 1818 with John Ross. They admired Parry; over-all, however, they viewed the British discovery expeditions—in ships that were ice-strengthened to a fare-thee-well, manned by inexperienced crews and commanded by officers seeking "imperishable renown"—as a pompous exercise in state politics, of little or no practical value.

Men and officers alike would have mused more on the blubber and bone below decks, for *that* was tangible wealth. These two parts of just a single whale would sell on the docks at Hull for ten to fifteen times what a man could expect to make in a year's work ashore.

The men on the decks, dozing in the sun on their day off, likely had no thought at all of how utterly devastating their way of life would prove to the Eskimo and the bowhead. They felt, instead, a sense of fortune. And they yearned for home.

The Canadian historian W. Gillies Ross cautiously suggests that as many as 38,000 Greenland right whales may have been killed in the Davis Strait fishery, largely by the British fleet. A sound estimate of the size of that population today is 200. There are no similar figures for the number of native people in the region who fell to diphtheria, small-pox, tuberculosis, poliomyelitis, and other diseases—historians have suggested that 90 percent of the indigenous population of North America is not an unreasonable figure. The Eskimos are still trying, as it were, to recover.★

★"Eskimo" is an inclusive term, referring to descendants of the Thule cultural tradition in present-day Canada and the Punuk and Birnirk cultural traditions in modern-day Alaska.

What happened around Pond's Bay in the heyday of arctic whaling represents in microcosm the large-scale advance of Western culture into the Arctic. It is a disquieting reminder that the modern industries—oil, gas, and mineral extraction—might be embarked on a course as disastrously short-lived as was that of the whaling industry. And as naive—our natural histories of this region 150 years later are still cursory and unintegrated. This time around, however, the element in the ecosystem at greater risk is not the bowhead but the coherent vision of an indigenous people. We have no alternative, long-lived narrative to theirs, no story of human relationships with that landscape independent of Western science and any desire to control or possess. Our intimacy lacks historical depth, and is still largely innocent of what is obscure and subtle there.

And our conceptions of its ultimate value vary markedly. The future disposition of the Arctic is not viewed in the same way by a Montreal attorney working on the settlement of Inuit land claims and by a naval architect in Sweden designing an ice-breaking tanker capable of plying the polar route from Rotterdam to Yokohama. And the life history of the Arctic—the pollination of its flowers by the bumblebee, the origins and thoughts of the Dorset people, the habits of the wolverine—means one thing to an *inuk* pulling on his fishnets at the mouth of the Hayes River, another to a biologist watching a caribou herd encounter the trans-Alaska pipeline, and yet something else to the modern tourist, bound for a caviar-and-champagne luncheon at the North Pole.

Such a variety of human views and interests in an emerging land is not new; what is new for us, and troubling, is a difference in the land itself, which changes the very nature of these considerations. In the Temperate Zone, we are accustomed to dealing with landscapes that can easily accommodate opposing views. Their long grow-ing seasons, mild temperatures, great variety of creatures, and moderate rainfall make up for much human abuse. The biological nature of arctic ecosystems is different—they are far more vulnerable ecologically to attempts to "accom-modate both sides." Of concern in the North, then, is the impatience with which reconciliation and compromise are now being sought.

Our conceptual problems with these things, with com-mercial and industrial development in the North and with the proprieties of an imposed economics there, can be traced to a fundamental strangeness in the landscape itself, to something as subtle as our own temperate-zone predilec-tion toward a certain duration and kind of light. Or for the particular shape that time takes in a temperate land, where the sun actually sets on a summer evening, where cicadas give way in the twilight to crickets, and people sit on porches—none of which happens in the Arctic.

Difficulty in evaluating, or even discerning, a particular landscape is related to the distance a culture has traveled from its own ancestral landscape. As temperate-zone people, we have long been ill-disposed toward deserts and expanses of tundra and ice. They have been wastelands for us; historically we have not cared at all what happened in them or to them. I am inclined to think, however, that their value will one day prove to be inestimable to us. It is precisely because the regimes of light and time in the Arc-tic are so different that this landscape is able to expose in startling ways the complacency of our thoughts about land in general. Its unfamiliar rhythms point up the narrow impetuosity of Western schedules, by simply changing the basis of the length of the day. And the periodically frozen Arctic Ocean is at present an insurmountable impediment to timely shipping. This land, for some, is irritatingly and uncharacteristically uncooperative.

If we are to devise an enlightened plan for human activity in the Arctic, we need a more particularized understanding of the land itself—not a more refined mathematical knowledge but a deeper understanding of its nature, as if it were, itself, another sort of civilization we had to reach some agreement with. I would draw you, therefore, back to the concrete dimensions of the land and to what they precipitate; simply to walk across the tundra; to watch the wind stirring a little in the leaves of dwarf birch and willows; to hear the hoof-clacket of migrating caribou. Imagine your ear against the loom of a kayak paddle in the Beaufort Sea, hearing the long, quivering tremolo voice of the bearded seal. Or feeling the surgical sharpness of an Eskimo's obsidian tool under the stroke of your finger.

Once in winter I was far out on the sea ice north of Melville Island in the high Arctic with a drilling crew. I saw a seal surface at some hourless moment in the day in a moon pool, the open water directly underneath the drilling platform that lets the drill string pass through the ice on its way to the ocean floor. The seal and I regarded each other in absolute stillness, I in my parka, arrested in the middle of an errand, the seal in the motionless water, its dark brown eyes glistening in its gray, catlike head. Curiosity held it. What held me was: how far out on the edge of the world I am. A movement of my head shifted the hood of my parka slightly, and the seal was gone in an explosion of water. Its eyes had been enormous. I walked to the edge of the moon pool and stared into the dark ocean. I could not have been more surprised by the seal's appearance if it had fallen out of the winter sky overhead, into the spheres of light that embraced the drill rig and our isolated camp.

To contemplate what people are doing out here and ignore the universe of the seal, to consider human quest and plight and not know the land, I thought, to not listen to it, seemed fatal. Not perhaps for tomorrow, or next year, but fatal if you looked down the long road of our determined evolution and wondered at the considerations that had got us this far.

At the heart of this narrative, then, are three themes: the influence of the arctic landscape on the human imagination. How a desire to put a landscape to use shapes our evaluation of it. And, confronted by an unknown landscape, what happens to our sense of wealth. What does it mean to grow rich? Is it to have red-blooded adventures and to make a fortune, which is what brought the whalers and other entrepreneurs north? Or is it, rather, to have a good family life and to be imbued with a far-reaching and intimate knowledge of one's homeland, which is what the Tununirmiut told the whalers at Pond's Bay wealth was? Is it to retain a capacity for awe and astonishment in our lives, to continue to hunger after what is genuine and worthy? Is it to live at moral peace with the universe?

It is impossible to know, clearly, the answer to this question; but by coming to know a place where the common elements of life are understood differently one has the advantage of an altered perspective. With that shift, it is possible to imagine afresh the way to a lasting security of the soul and heart, and toward an accommodation in the flow of time we call history, ours and the world's.

That dream, as it unfolds in the following chapters, is the dream of great and common people alike.

THE NATURALIST

My home stands on a wooded bench, set back about two hundred feet from the north bank of the McKenzie River in western Oregon. Almost every day I go down to the river with no intention but to sit and watch. I have been watching the river for thirty years, just the three or four hundred yards of it I can see from the forested bank, a run of clear, quick water about 350 feet wide. If I have learned anything here, it's that each time I come down, something I don't know yet will reveal itself.

If it's a man's intent to spend thirty years staring at a river's environs in order to arrive at an explanation of the river, he should find some other way to spend his time. To assert this, that a river can't be known, does not to my way of thinking denigrate science, any more than saying a brown bear can't be completely known. The reason this is true is because the river is not a thing, in the way a Saturn V rocket engine is a thing. It is an expression of biological life, in dynamic relation to everything around it—the salmon within, the violet-green swallow swooping its surface, alder twigs floating its current, a mountain lion sipping its bank water, the configurations of basalt that break its flow and give it timbre and tone.

In my experience with field biologists, those fresh to a task—say, caracara research—are the ones most likely to give themselves a deadline—ten years, say—against which they will challenge themselves to know all there is to know about that falcon. It never works. More seasoned field biologists, not as driven by a need to prove themselves, are content to concentrate on smaller arenas of knowledge. Instead of speaking definitively of coyote, armadillo, or wigeon, they tend to say, "This one animal, that one time, did this in that place." It's the approach to nature many hunting and gathering peoples take, to this day. The view suggests a horizon rather than a boundary for knowing, toward which we are always walking.

A great shift in the Western naturalist's frame of mind over the past fifty years, it seems to me, has been the growth of this awareness: to get anywhere deep with a species, you must immerse yourself in its milieu. You must study its ecology. If you wish to understand the caracara, you need to know a great deal about exactly where the caracara lives when; and what the caracara's relationships are with each of the many components of that place, including its weathers, its elevations, its seasonal light.

A modern naturalist, then, is no longer someone who goes no further than a stamp collector, mastering nomenclature and field marks. She or he knows a local flora and fauna as pieces of an inscrutable mystery, increasingly deep, a unity of organisms Western culture has been trying to elevate itself above since at least Mesopotamian times. The modern naturalist, in fact, has now become a kind of emissary in this, working to reestablish good relations with all the biological components humanity has excluded from its moral universe.

Sitting by the river, following mergansers hurtling past a few inches off its surface or eyeing an otter hauled out on a boulder with (in my binoculars) the scales of a trout glistening on its face, I ask myself not: What do I know?—that Canada geese have begun to occupy the nests of osprey here in recent springs, that harlequin ducks are now expanding their range to include this stretch of the river— but: Can I put this together? Can I imagine the river as a definable entity, evolving in time?

How is a naturalist today supposed to imagine the place between nature and culture? How is he or she to act, believing as many do that Western civilization is compromising its own biology by investing so heavily in material progress? And knowing that many in positions of corporate and political power regard nature as inconvenient, an inefficiency in their plans for a smoothly running future?

The question of how to behave, it seems to me, is nerve-racking to contemplate because it is related to two areas of particular discomfort for naturalists. One is how to keep the issue of spirituality free of religious commentary; the other is how to manage emotional grief and moral indignation in pursuits so closely tied to science, with its historical claim to objectivity.

One response to the first concern is that the naturalist's spirituality is one with no icons (unlike religion's), and it is also one that enforces no particular morality. In fact, for many it is not much more than the residue of awe which modern life has not (yet) erased, a sensitivity to the realms of life which are not yet corraled by dogma. The second concern, how a person with a high regard for objectivity deals with emotions like grief and outrage, like so many questions about the trajectory of modern culture, is only a request to express love without being punished. It is, more deeply, an expression of the desire that love be on an equal footing with power when it comes to social change.

It is of some help here, I think, to consider where the modern naturalist has come from, to trace her or his ancestry. Since the era of Gilbert White in eighteenth-century England, by some reckonings, we have had a recognizable cohort of people who study the natural world and write about it from personal experience. White and his allies wrote respectfully about nature, and their treatments were meant to be edifying for the upper classes. Often, the writer's intent was merely to remind the reader not to overlook natural wonders, which were the evidence of Divine creation. Darwin, in his turn, brought unprecedented depth to this kind of work. He accentuated the need for scientific rigor in the naturalist's inquiries, but he also suggested that certain far-reaching implications existed. Entanglements. People, too, he said, were biological, subject to the same forces of mutation as the finch. A hundred years further on, a man like Aldo Leopold could be characterized as a keen observer, a field biologist who understood a deeper connection (or reconnection) with nature, but also as someone aware of the role wildlife science had begun to play in politics. With Rachel Carson, the artificial but sometimes dramatic divide that can separate the scientist, with her allegiance to objective, peer-reviewed data, from the naturalist, for whom biology always raises issues of propriety, becomes apparent.

Following Leopold's and Carson's generations came a generation of naturalists that combined White's enthusiasm and sense of the nonmaterial world; Leopold's political consciousness and feelings of shared fate; and Carson's sense of rectitude and citizenship. For the first time, however, the humanists among this cadre of naturalists were broadly educated in the sciences. They had grown up with Watson and Crick, not to mention sodium fluoroacetate, Ebola virus ecology, melting ice shelves, and the California condor.

The modern naturalist, acutely, even depressingly, aware of the planet's shrinking and eviscerated habitats, often feels compelled to do more than merely register the damage. The impulse to protest, however, is often stifled by feelings of defensiveness, a fear of being misread. Years of firsthand field observation can be successfully challenged in court today by a computer modeler with not an hour's experience in the field. A carefully prepared analysis of stream flow, migration corridors, and long-term soil stability in a threatened watershed can be written off by the press (with some assistance from the opposition) as a hatred of mankind.

At the opening of the twenty-first century the naturalist, then, knows an urgency White did not foresee and a political scariness Leopold might actually have imagined in his worst moments. Further, in the light of the still-unfolding lessons of Charles Darwin's work, he or she knows that a cultural exemption from biological imperatives remains in the realm of science fiction.

In contemporary native villages, one might posit today that all people actively engaged in the land—hunting, fishing, gathering, traveling, camping—are naturalists, and say that some are better than others according to their gifts of observation. Native peoples differ here, however, from the Gilbert Whites, the Darwins, the Leopolds, and the Rachel Carsons in that accumulating and maintaining this sort of information is neither avocation nor profession. It is more comparable to religious activity, behavior steeped in tradition and considered essential for the maintenance of good living. It is a moral and an inculcated stance, a way of being. While White and others, by contrast, were searching for a way back in to nature, native peoples (down to the present in some instances), for whatever reason, have been at pains not to leave. The distinction is important because "looking for a way back in" is a striking characteristic of the modern naturalist's frame of mind.

Gilbert White stood out among his social peers because what he pursued—a concrete knowledge of the natural world around Selbourne in Hampshire—was unrelated to politics or progress. As such, it could be dismissed politically. Fascinating stuff, but inconsequential. Since then, almost every naturalist has borne the supercilious judgments of various sophisticates who thought the naturalist a romantic, a sentimentalist, a bucolic—or worse; and more latterly, the condescension of some scientists who thought the naturalist not rigorous, not analytic, not detached enough.

A naturalist of the modern era—an experientially based, well-versed devotee of natural ecosystems—is ideally among the best informed of the American electorate when it comes to the potentially catastrophic environmental effects of political decisions. The contemporary naturalist, it has turned out—again, scientifically grounded, politically attuned, field experienced, library enriched—is no custodian of irrelevant knowledge, no mere adept differentiating among Empidonax flycatchers on the wing, but a kind of citizen whose involvement in the political process, in the debates of public life, in the evolution of literature and the arts, has become crucial.

The bugbear in all of this—and there is one—is the role of field experience, the degree to which the naturalist's assessments are empirically grounded in firsthand knowledge. How much of what the contemporary naturalist claims to know about animals and the ecosystems they share with humans derives from what he has read, what he has heard, what he has seen televised? What part of what the naturalist has sworn his or her life to comes from firsthand experience, from what the body knows?

One of the reasons native people still living in some sort of close, daily association with their ancestral lands are so fascinating to those who arrive from the rural, urban, and suburban districts of civilization is because they are so possessed of authority. They radiate the authority of firsthand encounters. They are storehouses of it. They have not read about it, they have not compiled notebooks and assembled documentary photographs. It is so important that they remember it. When you ask them for specifics, the depth of what they can offer is scary. It's scary because it's not tidy, it doesn't lend itself to summation. By the very way that they say that they know, they suggest they are still learning something that cannot, in the end, be known.

It is instructive to consider how terrifying certain inter-lopers—rural developers, government planners, and other apostles of change—can seem to such people when, on the basis of a couple of books the interloper has read or a few (usually summer) weeks in the field with a pair of binoc-ulars and some radio collars, he suggests a new direction for the local ecosystem and says he can't envision any diffi-culties.

In all the years I have spent standing or sitting on the banks of this river, I have learned this: the more knowl-edge I have, the greater becomes the mystery of what holds that knowledge together, this reticulated miracle called an ecosystem. The longer I watch the river, the more amazed I become (afraid, actually, sometimes) at the confidence of those people who after a few summer sea-sons here are ready to tell the county commissioners, emphatically, what the river is, to scribe its meaning for the outlander.

Firsthand knowledge is enormously time-consuming to acquire; with its dallying and lack of end points, it is also out of phase with the short-term demands of modern life. It teaches humility and fallibility, and so represents an antithesis to progress. It makes a stance of awe in the wit-ness of natural process seem appropriate, and attempts at summary knowledge naïve. Historically, tyrants have sought selectively to eliminate firsthand knowledge when its sources lay outside their control. By silencing those with problem-atic firsthand experiences, they reduced the number of potential contradictions in their political or social designs, and so they felt safer. It is because natural process—how a mountain range disintegrates or how nitrogen cycles through a forest—is beyond the influence of the visionaries of globalization that firsthand knowledge of a country's ecosystems, a rapidly diminishing pool of expertise and awareness, lies at the radical edge of any country's political thought.

Over the years I have become a kind of naturalist, although I previously rejected the term because I felt I did not know enough, that my knowledge was far too incomplete. I never saw myself in the guise of Gilbert White, but I respected his work enough to have sought out his grave in Selbourne and expressed there my gratitude for his life. I never took a course in biology, not even in high school, and so it seemed to me that I couldn't really be any sort of authentic naturalist. What biology I was able to learn I took from books, from veterinary clinics, from an apprenticeship to my homeland in the Cascades, from field work with Western biologists, and from traveling with hunters and gatherers. As a naturalist, I have taken the lead of native tutors, who urged me to participate in the natural world, not hold it before me as an object of scrutiny.

When I am by the river, therefore, I am simply there. I watch it closely, repeatedly, and feel myself not apart from it. I do not feel compelled to explain it. I wonder sometimes, though, whether I am responding to the wrong question when it comes to speaking "for nature." Perhaps the issue is not whether one has the authority to claim to be a naturalist, but whether those who see themselves as naturalists believe they have the authority to help shape the world. What the naturalist-as-emissary intuits, I think, is that if he or she doesn't speak out, the political debate will be left instead to those seeking to benefit their various constituencies. Strictly speaking, a naturalist has no constituency.

To read the newspapers today, to merely answer the phone, is to know the world is in flames. People do not have time for the sort of empirical immersion I believe crucial to any sort of wisdom. This terrifies me, but I, too, see the developers' bulldozers arrayed at the mouth of every canyon, poised at the edge of every plain. And the elimination of these lands, I know, will further reduce the extent of the blueprints for undamaged life. After the last undomesticated stretch of land is brought to heel, there will be only records—strips of film and recording tape, computer printouts, magazine articles, books, laser-beam surveys—of these immensities. And then any tyrant can tell us what it meant, and in which direction we should now go. In this scenario, the authority of the grizzly bear will be replaced by the authority of a charismatic who says he represents the bear. And the naturalist—the ancient emissary to a world civilization wished to be rid of, a world it hoped to transform into a chemical warehouse, the same uneasy emissary who intuited that to separate nature from culture wouldn't finally work—will be an orphan. He will become a dealer in myths.

What being a naturalist has come to mean to me, sitting my mornings and evenings by the river, hearing the clack of herons through the creak of swallows over the screams of osprey under the purl of fox sparrows, so far removed from White and Darwin and Leopold and even Carson, is this: Pay attention to the mystery. Apprentice to the best apprentices. Rediscover in nature your own biology. Write and speak with appreciation for all you have been gifted. Recognize that a politics with no biology, or a politics without field biology, or a political platform in which human biological requirements form but one plank, is a vision of the gates of Hell.

THE ENTREATY
OF THE WIIDEEMA

I should preface my remarks this evening—and I must say that this will not be an entirely hopeful talk, and for that I apologize—with some explanations of how I came to live with—to try to live with, really—the Wiideema.

When I finished my doctoral studies among the Navajo of the American Southwest, I realized, as many students do, that I knew less at the end than I did in the beginning. That is, so much of what I took to be the objective truth when I started—things as self-evident, say, as Copernicus's arrangement of the inner planets—became so diluted by being steeped in another epistemology that simultaneously I came to grasp the poverty of my own ideas and the eternity of paradox within Navajo thought.

Let me put this to you in another way. When I finished my work among the Navajo—or, to be both more precise and more honest, when I gave up among the Navajo—I had as my deepest wish that someone among them would have been studying my way of knowing the world. I might have been more capable then of accepting the Navajo as true intellectual companions, and not, as has happened to so many of us, have ended up feeling disillusionment, even despair, with my own culture. I believe I would have been able to grasp *our* expression of Beauty Way, and in that sense I would have fallen back in love with my own people.

But it did not work this way. My postdoctoral studies brought me here, to Austin, where I declared I wanted to look at something I'd never studied before—among people I'd have to go out and *find,* an undiscovered people. On the strength of my work with the Navajo—and, again, to be candid with you, although I learned to speak that extremely difficult language fluently and though, for example, I memorized the full nine days of Blessing Way prayers, the obsession cost me my marriage, my two children—on the strength of that earlier work, I was granted awards and fellowships by the Wenner-Gren Foundation, the Kellogg Foundation, the University of Texas at Austin, and the Henry Solomon Memorial Trust. This financial support, and the regard with which my own department treated me—my teaching duties here were light to begin with, and I must acknowledge, embarrassing as it is, that I *took* them lightly—with all this underpinning, I set out to find a tribe of people with whom I could explore one idea—hunting.

The conventional wisdom on this, of course, is that there are no intact hunting cultures left in the wilder Southern Hemisphere—not in Africa, not in South America, not in Australia. I'd learned through a friend, however, that it was possible a few, small hunting bands might still exist uncontacted in the Western Desert, in Australia. So I went there immediately. I'll be brief about this part of it. An important question—Why disturb these people if they are, indeed, there?—was one I deliberately ignored. I suppressed it, I will tell you, with a terrible intellectual strength. I importuned every professional acquaintance, until I got myself so well situated in the anthropological community I was able to arrange a small expedition, with the approval of the Central (Aboriginal) Land Council, into a region of Western Australia west of the Tanami Desert, where I was most hopeful of contacting a relict hunting band. It is now safe, though still compromising, to reveal that I lied to arrange this expedition, both to my friends and to the Land Council. I was not interested, as I claimed, in searching out the last refuges of rare marsupial animals and in comparing what I could learn of their biology and ecology with information gathered in conversations with local people and gleaned from scholarly publications on their hunting practices, belief systems, myths. I wanted to find a fresh people, and to pursue with them another idea.

When the Wiideema, in fact, found *us*—in the Northern Territory, technically, not in Western Australia, though the designation of course meant nothing to them—I was ecstatic. As soon as I realized the Wiideema were shadowing us—a fact I was the last to discover, though I believed I was the first—I contrived to abandon my white companions and our aboriginal guides. Under cover of darkness one night I simply walked out of camp. I'd not gone but a mile before I felt the presence, the subtle pressure, of other people. And there they were, standing like so many dark sticks in the sand among tufts of spinifex grass. Truly, it was as though they had materialized.

I made signs that I very much wished to join them and leave my companions. We walked that night until I was delirious with exhaustion. We slept the whole of the next day in the shade of some boulders, walked all the following night, and then did the same again, another two days. My exhaustion turned to impatience, impatience to anger, anger to despair, and despair to acquiescence. In this manner I was bled.

Through it all I took notes, most especially on hunting. My position during those first few weeks, however, could be construed as that of a camp dog. I was given scraps to eat, patted on the shoulder by some of the older women, was yelled at, and served as a source of laughter when performing ordinary tasks—making a double-secure tie in the laces of my boots, for example, or when I examined the binding on a spear shaft with a hand lens.

One day, having had more than my fill of this and being the butt of pranks—the children sniped at me in the same way their parents did, a probing but ultimately indifferent curiosity—I confronted one of the men, Karratumanta, and with a look of defiant exasperation burned a smoking hole in a eucalyptus limb with my hand glass. Karratumanta regarded me blankly. He picked up a stone and threw it with terrific force at a small bird flying by. The stone knocked the bird, a songlark, to the ground, dead. He stripped away and ate its two minute slabs of pectoral flesh and then regarded me as though I were crazy to assume superiority.

You can imagine how this played out, certainly, in those first weeks. On reflection, I realized my plans had probably been transparent to my white companions and to our guides, and that they had no intention at all of searching for me. Instead, they trusted little harm and some good would come from my conceits and lack of integrity. I hope, in the end, you will find that they were correct.

In the early days of my work with the Wiideema—I call it "my work" because it was work, keeping up with them—I was dazzled, predictably, by the startling degree of their intimacy with the places we traveled through. The capacity of every object, from a mountain range to an insect gall, to hold an idea or to abet human life was known to them. I expected this high level of integration with place, a degree of belonging that the modern world envies, perhaps too desperately; but I was not prepared for the day I began to hear English words in their conversations. The first words I heard were "diptych," "quixotic," and "effervesce," words sufficiently obscure to have seemed Wiideema expressions, accented and set off in the run of conversation exactly as they would be in English. But they were not Wiideema words. Over a period of days I began to hear more and more English, not just words but phrases and occasionally entire sentences. What was happening was so strange that I did not want to ask about it. During my years in the field, if I have learned one thing, it is not to ask the obvious question right away. Wait, and you often see the whole event more clearly.

When I could understand almost everything that was being said, though in a way I'd never understood English before, I asked Yumbultjaturra, one of the women, "Where did you learn to speak English?"

"What is that, 'English,' the name of your language?"

"It's what we're speaking."

"No, no," she said smiling. "We are merely speaking. You, *you,* I think, might be speaking that."

"But we can understand each other. How could we understand each other if we both weren't speaking English?"

"We can understand each other because—how should I put this to you?—we do not have a foreign language. You understand what I say, don't you?"

"Yes."

"At first you didn't."

"Right, yes."

"However," she said, "from the beginning we understood you."

"From the start? Then why did you never answer my questions, why didn't you speak to me?"

"We spoke to you all the time," she stated. "And forgive me, but your questions were not compelling. And to be truthful, no one was inclined to speak with you until you put your questions away. You'd have to say this is a strict tenet with us—listening."

Our conversation went on in this manner for five or ten minutes before I understood what she was doing. She wasn't, in fact, speaking English. It was not even correct to say that she was speaking Wiideema. She was just speaking, the way a bird speaks or a creek, as a fish speaks or wind rushes in the grass. If I became anxious listening to her, she got harder to understand. The more I tried to grapple with our circumstances, the less I was able to converse. Eventually, in order to understand and be understood, I simply accepted the fact that we could understand each other.

Now, knowing this, I can imagine what you are perhaps anticipating—but it did not happen. I had no intellectual discussion with the people I traveled with. We did not dis-

cuss or compare cosmologies. I did not seek to discover
whether the grand metaphors of my own culture—entropy,
let us say, or the concept of husbandry—had their counter-
parts in Wiideema culture. I did not pursue any philosophical issues with them, say Gandhi's ahimsa, or the possibility
of universal justice. No Enlightenment notions of universal human dignity. I simply traveled. I drew the country into
myself, very much as I drew air into my lungs. Or drank
water. I ceased what finally seemed to me my infernal
questions and menacing curiosity. And I finally came to see
the Wiideema as a version of something of which my own
people were a version. What we shared—and it was a source
of pleasure as intense as any I had ever known—was not
solely food and common hearth, human touch, small gifts,
things I would have expected, but a sense of danger. A sense
that it was dangerous to be alive.

I do not mean by such danger poisonous snakes or no
water; or solely that you might be bludgeoned in your
sleep, all of which occurred. The sense of danger we
shared came from accepting consciousness. Human consciousness beckons us all. My Wiideema companions, wary
as wild animals, had not accepted it fully. They didn't shun
knowledge; and it was not that they were never contem-
plative or curious about ideas or other abstractions. But
their hesitancy had led them off in another direction. All
that they knew, all they believed or imagined, they cast in
stories. Stories for them were the only safe containers for
what consciousness, as we have it, might have elucidated
for them about life. Or let me say this another way. When I
put my imagination, as distinct from my intellect, together

with their stories, having steeped my body in the food, the water, light, wind, and sand of the Wiideema, I found as much in these stories as I could expect to find in the most profound and beautiful Occidental articulation of any idea or event with which I am familiar.

I finally left the Wiideema—a decision awful and hard to arrive at—because I could not exercise the indifference they managed toward violence. On several occasions, the fourteen people I traveled with encountered other groups. Often these encounters were friendly, but three times they were fatally violent. Someone was murdered. And then life started over again. In a troubling way this was like hunting. An animal was killed and eaten, and all were refreshed. The distinction, the emotional and moral separation between human and animal death, was one I could never grasp in my Occidental mind and not perceive in my infant Wiideema mind. They were willing to accept far more suffering in their lives—from heat, from starvation, from thirst, from wounds—than I could abide. And nothing but thoughts of retribution, as far as I knew, were raised for them by incidents of murder.

In the end, I did not consider that the Wiideema lived on some lower plane, or, transcendent in their infinitely clever world of stories, that they lived on a higher plane. I thought of them as companions on the same plane, shielding themselves in a different way from the fatal paradoxes of life.

When I left the Wiideema it was in the same fashion as I had arrived, rising in the night and walking away, though I understood now this was only a ritual, that my departure was not camouflaged. I had learned enough to get on alone in the desert, unless circumstances became truly dire. I walked out at Yinapaka, a perennial lake in the outwash of the Lander River, and eventually met some Warlpiri people who took me to Willowra. From there I came home.

What I hoped to find when I left Austin two and a half years ago was an uncontacted people with whom I could study the hunting of animals. I was curious about how, emotionally and spiritually—if you will allow me that imprecise word—people accustom themselves to daily killing, to the constant taking of life, as I saw it. I was afraid that in my dealings with the Navajo, a people studied nearly to death, all I was learning was a version of what I or others already knew. What I found when I began to travel with the Wiideema was that their emotions, their spiritual nature, were unknowable. When we killed and roasted kangaroo, I could only inquire into my own ethics, question my own emotions. I sought, finally, companionship with the Wiideema, not reason, not explanation.

I have to say, however odd it may sound, that what little true knowledge I returned with is knowledge already known to us—that we and the Wiideema share the same insoluble difficulties, which each day we must abide. And that not "once" but *now* is a time when human beings all speak the same language. (What actually happens, I think, is that people simply speak their own language but it is clearly understood by each listener.)

I wanted, two and a half years ago, to gain another kind

of knowledge, the wisdom, so named, of primitive people. One day my friend Karratumanta killed a man called Ketjimidji. He speared him quickly through the lungs without warning. There were six or seven of us standing together when it happened. We had met on a trail, Ketjimidji's people coming from a soak or water hole and our group walking toward it. No voices were raised. No argument broke out. The killing—Karratumanta handled Ketjimidji deftly, coolly, on the spear, until Ketjimidji went down and stopped struggling—was followed by a preternatural silence. Ketjimidji's people went away, carrying the body with them, and we walked ahead to the soak. In the moments right after the killing I was fine but soon I was fighting for air. I felt as if all the bones in my face had exploded.

Ngatijimpa, one of Karratumanta's daughters, came to me that night and told me a story. It had nothing to do, as far as I could see, with what had happened. It was one of a long series of stories about the travels of Pakuru, the golden bandicoot. She was not, I finally understood, offering me allegory or explanation, but only a story, which, as she intended, pulled the sense of horror out of me in some mysterious way. I slept. But I remembered. And my nights afterward were disturbed because I remembered. I couldn't be healed of it, if that is the right word.

Karratumanta, a tutor of mine, had seen me reeling after the spearing and said, "I will not be your martyr."

Many months later I was spattered by blood when another person was killed violently in front of me. Again, Ngatijimpa came to me. She told me another part of the story of Pakuru and his travels and under the soothe of the story I slept deeply. Ngatijimpa was young, only a girl, but she was eloquent and effective with the wisdom she dispensed.

I owe those who have supported me an exact and detailed report of my months with the Wiideema, a scholarly work rigorous in its observations, well researched, cautious in its conclusions. I have begun this paper, and, somewhat to my surprise, I have made progress. In it I'm describing hunting techniques, the ethology of desert animals; but what I am really wondering, night and day, is what I can give the Wiideema. Such questions of allegiance seize upon us all I believe—how can we reciprocate, and how do we honor the unspoken request of our companions to speak the truth? What I wish to do here, the task-in-return I have set myself, is to rewrite the story of Cain. I want to find a language for it that offers hope in place of condemnation, that turns not on aggression and vengeance, but on the mystery of human terror.

I do not know if I will be successful, or—if I am—whether success will mean anything substantial. But having sojourned with the Wiideema, I want to understand now what it means to provide.

TEAL CREEK

In the Magdalena Mountains east of Ordell, in country that's been called the Bennett River country since the time of white people, an anchorite (as I would later come to understand the word) settled. His name was James Teal. He drove in when trillium were in full flower, April of 1954, in a green 1946 Dodge and stayed first for several weeks at the Courtyard Motel in Ordell before moving up onto the Bennett.

He brought no remarkable possessions. He walked with a slight limp, which my father thought might be from a war wound. He was tall, lean, his face vaguely Asiatic. I remember people noticed right away that he was not an intruder, and was easy to speak to. For a stranger who didn't have a job, or a way of life that fit him anywhere, he drew remarkably little suspicion in Ordell. Days, he was out of town in his car—people saw him walking in and out of the woods at different places; evenings he spent around the motel. He ate supper at Dan and Ruella's cafe or the Vincent Hotel. He didn't go into the bars. He bought groceries, like everyone, at Clyde's on Assiniboine—that's long gone now—and bought rope and pipe and things at Cassidy's Feed, which had a hardware section back then.

People like my father who always watched everything just a little said they saw less of him as summer went on. I don't remember, really, seeing much of him myself. I was infatuated with Esther Matthews and I missed a lot then, I suppose. But by the end of summer, August, he was gone.

After that, from the winter of '54–'55 on, he lived up on the Bennett. He gave the Dodge over to Wilton Haskin, who owned the Courtyard—some say he traded the car for rent or tools or meals, but if he did it was Wilton who likely got the better end of the deal. Wilton drove the car until he died in the fall of 1975. Then his son Clarence drove it another ten years.

Teal lived in two places I knew of on tributaries off the Bennett. One was at Cougar Creek and the other was on Lesley Creek, though for some reason then we called it White Dog Creek and now, like myself, some people call it Teal Creek.

Teal understood very well how to get on alone up there. He found spots where hot springs surfaced near south-facing benches, where he had light enough for a garden—which meant he looked the country over more closely than anyone I ever knew, or heard of. I was only inside the second cabin he built, but the first one must have been much like it, tight and simple. He broke and moved a lot of rock at the second place, a terrible amount of work, really, to make a good foundation for a one-room cabin. And he built a flume there at the second place, a wood chute to carry the flow of water from the hot spring through at floor level. He packed a woodstove in and had creek water, and he built a porch big enough to cover some of his firewood and a daybed.

I was thirteen the summer he moved up on Cougar Creek. I didn't go up that way to hunt or wander or fool around. No one did. At the time all the country around there was so open, so empty of people, no one much kept him in mind. He wasn't any trespasser. It was all federal land. We would see him in town once or twice, early in the spring or late in summer. He'd work a few weeks for Wilton, buy staples at Clyde's, and then hitch back out to Bennett River. From the highway he'd walk up Cougar Creek to his place or, later, the four miles up White Dog Creek.

Those times he'd hitch back out of town, once I got my license, I'd think about offering him a ride. He was the most beguiling person to me, beckoning, like the first pungent smell of cottonwood buds. He seemed as independent and benign as the moon. But I was shy and my father disapproved of that kind of curiosity.

I went away to college in '59. Summers I worked with my father, a heavy-equipment contractor. In the summer after my junior year we were building logging roads back up from the Bennett. One night, halfway home, I missed my wallet and turned the truck around, certain it had fallen out at the work site. I found it on the ground alongside the grader I was driving. By then it was after seven, but the sky was still bright, and I got to thinking about James Teal. Without knowing why, without really looking at what I was doing, I pulled off the road at Lesley Creek bridge and sat there. I wanted to see his place. I wanted to talk with him. Where did he come from? What sort of things did he work at? Did he have a family somewhere? I wondered if he was purely white, but I wouldn't admit to the rank curiosity, the willingness to invade his privacy. I'd never had a conversation with the man. I had no reason at all to be calling.

Still, that evening I went up the creek. Dusk was long enough to see by for a few hours and I carried a flashlight to come back. I walked along a deer trail, just a few yards into the trees, a narrow path cushioned with moss and fir needles. No stranger would guess a man occasionally passed there.

It was dark when I finally descried the cabin. I saw its angles silhouetted in trees against the sky. Teal was standing on the porch, looking into the woods, but not toward me. In hearth or candle light I saw he wore a white T-shirt tucked in his trousers and that he was barefoot. I squatted down on the trail. Two Swainson's thrushes were calling, back and forth. After a while they were quiet and Teal went in. I heard the door close, the metal latch fall.

I felt foolish and at the same time a little frightened. I'd come all this way, then said nothing, and had hidden from the man. I couldn't understand why I was scared, but I got so dizzy I had to sit. I felt myself in a kind of sinkhole in the darkness. I knew if I walked up to the cabin and spoke to him I'd be all right. But I turned back on the deer trail. My skin prickled. I ran fast, imagining feral dogs chasing me down. I tangled in limbs and blackberry vines. All the way out to the road I felt an edge of panic.

At the truck I calmed myself. It wasn't Teal that had frightened me. It wasn't the dark, either. What scared me was the thought that I might have injured him. I knew right then what it meant to trespass.

Late in the summer of 1967, I moved back to Ordell and went to work full-time for my father. I had married a woman named Julie Quiros from Stuart River. I'd finished four years in the army, none of it, I've always been grateful, in Vietnam, and we'd had a daughter, Blair. My mother's younger brother, despondent, involved with another woman, had shot himself and his wife, and their three children, all girls, had come to live with my parents. Clyde Brennan had closed his store and another market had opened up.

Teal, like the first wildly colored harlequin duck I ever saw, had been somewhere at the edge of my thoughts all that time, ever since that night. When I got home I asked my father if he'd seen him recently. He said yes, Teal had been in town that August, had worked a little for Wilton, the same as always, then he'd gone back out to his place—and certainly, whether it was federal land or not, it *was* his place by now.

What could he believe in? I wondered. What allowed him to be comfortable out there from one year to the next? Whatever his beliefs were, he didn't bother anybody with them. Whenever he came to town he got on easily with people. I remember even a few times he played softball with us, laughing as much as anyone when he dropped easy pop flies or struck out. Did he keep a tidy shelf of books up there? And which books would those be? Did he reel and crouch in the moon's light?

Though I'd never done so as a boy, I knew there were

spots along the Bennett good to swim in, and on an Indian summer day in September of '67 I took Julie and Blair up to a place past Teal Creek. They swam. I couldn't keep my attention on them. I felt my unseemly curiosity, the cowardice and insistence of it, and I knew Julie was aware that something was running in my mind.

I looked over at her, at the soft, veined line of her neck, where it rose from her shoulders.

"You know that fellow Teal?" I asked.

"The hermit?"

"I don't know, really." After a while I said, "When I was fourteen, a man named Ephraim Lincoln told all of us a story about Teal, one morning at Clyde's during hunting season. He said he found where Teal had walked barefoot in the snow and seen where he'd knelt down for a long time by a little waterfall, then lay out full, naked. I shook my head and laughed right along with the older men, but everyone knew that the scorn was wrong, misdirected. It was Ephraim who was lewd, a corrupt individual.

"Ever since then, I've known I wanted to protect Teal. And that I should—that I'm meant to—receive something from him. I don't know what it is."

Julie rested her fingers on my arm.

That fall instead of going up Enid River to look for deer with a friend I went alone up the Bennett. I planned to walk in along Cougar Creek and just roam around. If I saw Teal's first cabin, well, fine. I'd look it over. I knew I wouldn't shoot any deer up there, no matter. It would have been wrong, mixing those things.

I got about a mile up Cougar Creek and then knew I shouldn't be in there. I turned back, feeling a familiar dread and misgiving. Then, a short way down the trail, I was fine. It occurred to me that maybe Teal was dealing with menace, that out here he went chin to chin with an evil I could not imagine. The knowledge that he might do this shamed me. Where was my own courage, my own resolution?

That winter I began reading to Blair at night. We started off with fairy tales, but the most interesting stories to us after a while were Indian stories, ones collected by George Bird Grinnell and James Willard Schultz from Cheyenne and Blackfeet and Gros Ventre people not so far away, over in Montana and Wyoming. At first I thought Blair would be bored. The stories were mostly about young men traveling, or about the creation of the world. But she liked them. The stories were simple, without irony. They had a disarming morality to them that I enjoyed experiencing with her. When a story ended, Julie would hug us together and say, "And that's how the world really is. It's a true story." Later, when they'd gone to bed, I'd sit with some of the books and wonder about the Creation, and what it was, really, that kept the world from flying apart.

The year after I returned to Ordell my father had a heart attack and asked me to take over the business. Our lawyer drew up the papers and it was all done in a few days. My father had fifteen men working for him. I wasn't eager for the responsibility.

The following spring I decided to go visit Teal. One morning I just got in the truck and drove up the Bennett. If he asked me why I'd come I was going to say I didn't know. I felt bound to, I'd say. I wasn't going to make something up.

It was raining when I left the house and pouring by the

time I got to Teal Creek. I followed the deer trail all the way in to the cabin. From a clearing in front of the porch, another trail went between trees over a rise and out onto a treeless bench. I saw Teal standing out there in the downpour, beyond the green rows of a new garden. He was bent far over before the flat gray sky in what appeared to be an attitude of prayer or adoration, his arms at his sides. The rain had plastered his shirt to his back and his short black hair glistened. He did not move at all while I stood there, fifteen or twenty minutes. And in that time I saw what it was I had wanted to see all those years in James Teal. The complete stillness, a silence such as I had never heard out of another living thing, an unbroken grace. He was wound up in the world, neat and firm as a camas bulb in the ground, and spread out over it like three days of weather. The wind beat down on James Teal. Beyond him clouds snagged in the fir trees. The short growth in his garden between us was fresh and bright. When I turned to leave, the cabin looked lean, compact as a hunting heron.

That night when I lay with Julie I described the scene and told her the details, the history of my long desire to know James Teal, a desire that seemed, in that moment, to have abated. Two years later, on a balmy Saturday afternoon in May 1971, I again felt compelled to visit him, as though he had called to me from a dream. I found him slumped in a chair at an outside table, the remains of his lunch before him. Sparrows flew up from crumbs on the white porcelain plate. He had been dead only a few hours, I guessed.

I moved him over to the porch floor, laid him out there with his arms over his chest, and went inside to look for a blanket. I never before saw a room so obviously lived in, so hand and foot worn, so spare as that one. Beside the bed was a table and stool. The iron stove, a storage box, a single shelf with pans and dishes and some books. At one of the two windows was a sort of kneeler, which I later learned was called a prie-dieu.

I covered James Teal's body with a yellow blanket from his cot and walked out to the road. I sat there in the truck with the door propped open for a long time, reluctant to start the tasks that would bring the sheriff and the coroner and perhaps others up Teal Creek. We were reading a story just then, Julie and Blair and I, about how First Person was going to create bright, metallic dragonflies, cutthroat trout, short-eared owls, elk, and the other animals. I had not looked ahead as sometimes I do, but I imagined reading that evening about animals filling up the world. I imagined it would make us feel fine and grateful. Reading it aloud would make us feel as if nothing would go wrong.

THE WOMAN WHO HAD SHELLS

The light is blinding. The vast, flat beaches of Sanibel caught in the Caribbean noon are fired with a white belligerence, shells lying in such profusion that people unfamiliar arrive believing no one has ever been here.

The shells draw July heat from the languid air, shells brittle as Belleek, hard as stove bolts, with blushing, fluted embouchures, a gamut of watercolor pinks and blues. Shivering iridescence rises from abalone nacre. Hieroglyphics climb the walls of slender cones in spiraling brown lines. Conchs have the heft of stones. One shell hides both fists; others could be swallowed without discomfort, like pills. A form of genuflection turned over in the hand becomes a form of containment, its thin pastels the colors to chalk a prairie sunrise.

Here at dusk one afternoon, thinking I was alone, I took off a pair of pants, a light shirt, my shoes and shorts and lay down. On my back, arms outstretched, I probed the moist, cool surfaces beneath the sheet of white shells still holding the day's heat. I flexed and shifted against them until I lay

half buried, as if floating in saltwater. The afternoon trailed
from me. I was aware of a wisp of noise, like a waterfall
muffled in deep woods. The pulse of my own heart faded
and this sound magnified until in the mouths of the thousands of shells around and beneath me it became a wailing,
a keening as disarming, as real, as sudden high winds at sea.
It was into this moment—I remember opening my eyes
suddenly to see flamingos overhead, their lugubrious flight
etched against a lapis sky by the last shafts of light, the
murmuring glow of pale crimson in their feathered bel-
lies—into this moment that the woman stepped.

I turned my head to the side, ear pressed into the shells,
and saw her first at a great distance. I was drawn to her
immediately, to her tentative, cranelike movements, the
reach of her hand. I imagined her fingers as polite as the
waters of a slow and shallow creek, searching, sensitive
even to the colors of shells, the trace of spirits. She was
nearer now. With one movement she bent down and raised
two shells, scallops, and cupped them to her cheeks. I saw
clear in her face a look I have seen before only in the face
of a friend who paints, when he has finished, when the
mystery is established and accepted without explanation. I
held that connection in my mind even as she turned away,
knowing the chance these emotions were the same was
only slight, so utterly different are human feelings, but
believing we could, and do, live by such contrivance.

I wanted to speak out but could not move. She grew
smaller, touched one or two more places on the beach, like
an albatross trying to alight against a wind, took nothing
and disappeared.

I stared across the white expanse into the vault of the

evening sky, toward the emergence of the first stars. My
respect for her was without reason and profound. I lay for
hours unable to move. Whenever the urge to rise and dress
welled up, a sense of the density of the air, of one thought
slipping irretrievably off another into darkness overwhelmed
me. When finally I stood, I saw fields of shells around me
luminescent in the starlight. Near where my head had been
was a single flamingo feather. Across this landscape I made
my way home.

We carry such people with us in an imaginary way, proof
against some undefined but irrefutable darkness in the
world. The nimbus of that moment remained with me for
months. That winter, on a beach frozen to stone I stood
staring at the pack ice of the Arctic Ocean. The gray sea
ice gave way to gray sky in such a way that no horizon
could be found. In the feeble light my breath rolled out,
crystallized I knew on my eyebrows, on the fur at the edge
of my face. I wanted a memento. With my heel I began to
chip at the thin, wind-crusted snow on the sand. There
was a small shell, a blue and black mussel barely the length
of my fingernail. Stiff with the cold, I was able only with
great difficulty to maneuver it into a pocket of my parka,
and to zip it shut. I was dimly aware at that moment of the
woman, the turning of her skirt, extending her hand to the
shells on Sanibel Island.

In one of the uncanny accidents by which life is shaped, I
saw the woman the following year in New York. It was late

in winter. I saw her through a window, reaching for her water glass in a restaurant on West 4th Street, that movement.

It was early in the evening, hardly anyone there. I crossed the room and asked if I might sit down. She did not move. The expression in her face was unreadable. I recounted, as respectful of her privacy as I could be, how I had first seen her. She smiled and nodded acquiescence. For a moment I was not sure it was the same woman. She seemed veiled and unassuming.

She was a photographer, she said. She had been photographing in St. Petersburg when she went out that afternoon to Sanibel. I had been on vacation, I told her; I taught Asian history at the University of Washington—we found a common ground in Japan. A collection of her photographs of farms and rural life on the most northern island, Hokkaido, had just been published. I knew the book. In memory I saw images of cattle grazing in a swirling snowstorm, a weathered cart filled with a dimpled mound of grain, and birdlike hands gripping tools. In those first moments the images seemed a logical and graceful extension of her.

We talked for hours—about bumblebees and Cartier-Bresson, haiku, Tibet, and Western novels; and I asked if I could see her home. There was by then a warmth between us, but I could sense the edges of her privacy and would rather say good night, seal the evening here, hold that memory, than burden either of us. There is so much unfathomable in human beings; we so often intrude, meaning no harm, and injure for no reason. No, she said, she wouldn't mind at all.

We walked a great many blocks north, then east toward
the river. There was ice on the sidewalks and we linked
arms against it. Her apartment was a flat above weathered
storefronts. We sat on a couch in a spacious room painted
white, softly lit, with several large photographs on the wall,
of seagrass and of trees in a field in Michigan. I had
thought there would be shells somewhere in the room, but
there were not that I saw.

I began looking through one of her published books,
black-and-white photographs of rural Maine. She fixed a
gentle tea, like chamomile. We sipped tea. She was very
quiet and then she spoke about the shells. Whenever there
was time, she said, she went out looking. When she was in
Australia to work or in the Philippines, or on the coast of
Spain. When she first began she would collect them. Now
it was rare that she ever brought one home, even though
she continued to search, hoping especially to see a hypatian
murex and other shells that she might never find, or find
and leave. When she took vacations she used to go alone to
exotic beaches on the Coral and South China seas, and to
places like the Seychelles. Then, more and more, she stayed
home, going to Block Island or Martha's Vineyard, to
Assateague Island or to Padre Island in Texas, spending days
looking at the simplest whelks and clams, noting how very
subtly different they all were. The day I had seen her, she
said, was one of the times she had gone to Sanibel to walk,
to pick up a shell, turn it in the white tropical light, feel the
cusps and lines, and set it back. As she described what she
saw in the shells she seemed slowly to unfold. The movement of her hands to her teacup now had the same air of
reticence, of holy retrieval and graceful placement that I

had seen that day. She spoke of limpid waters, of unexpected colors, mikado yellow, cerulean blue, crimson flush, of their baroque and simple structure, their strength and fragility. Her voice was intimate, almost plaintive. When she stopped speaking it was very still.

The first pearling of light was visible on the window panes. After a long moment I walked quietly to where my coat lay and from a pocket took the small mussel shell from the Arctic coast. I returned to her. I said in the most subdued voice I could find where the shell had come from, and what it meant because of that day on Sanibel Island, and that I wished her to have it. She took it. What was now in the room I had no wish to disturb.

I crossed the room again to get my coat. She followed. At the door where I thought to try to speak there was a gentle pressure on my arm and she led me to the room where she slept. Her bed was on the floor. Two windows looked east over the city. By the bed was a small white table with a glass top set over what had once been a type drawer. In its compartments were shells.

She slid back the sheet of glass and sitting there on her heels she began to show them to me. In response to a question, she would say where a shell was from or the circumstances under which she had found it. Some were so thin I could see the color of my skin through them. Others were so delicately tinged I had to be told their color. They felt like bone, like water-worn glass and raw silk. Patterns like African fabric and inscriptions of Chinese characters. Cone shells like Ming vases. She turned my hand palm up and deposited in its depression what I at first thought were grains of sand. As my eye became accustomed to them I saw they were shells, that each one bore in infinitesimal precision a sunburst of fluting. The last she lay in my hands was like an egg, as white as alabaster and as smooth, save that its back was so intricately carved that my eye foundered in the detail.

She put the shells back and carefully replaced the glass. There was a kind of silence in the room that arrives only at dawn. Light broke the edge of a building and entered the window, bringing a glow to the pale curve of her neck. In the wall steam pipes suddenly hammered. Her hair moved, as if in response to breath, and I saw the flush outline of her cheek. In that stillness I heard her step among the shells at Sanibel and heard the pounding of wings overhead and imagined it was possible to let go of a fundamental anguish.

THE LETTERS OF HEAVEN

When I was a boy of thirteen I found a packet of letters in my father's desk. I picked the lock to the drawer one day with one of my mother's hairpins. Then, to keep my curiosity from being discovered, I took the small desk key one time when my father was sick, and in a distant quarter of Lima I had a stranger make a copy. That way I didn't run the risk, each time I opened the drawer, of mutilating the lock and having my sin exposed.

The letters had been written in Castilian Spanish in the first decade of the seventeenth century between a man and a woman who did not sign their names but who wrote in exquisite phrases of desire and anguish about their passion for each other. During the years I read and reread these letters, I thought them composed of the most beautiful and, at the same time, the most illicit of human statements. The language of enthrallment was so unrestrained that the images existed for me outside the realm of sin and redemption, beyond the sphere of the Church. Please understand the complication—sometimes in reading the words I found myself with a powerful erection, but I did not consider this state of excitement, the vibrating ventilation of my skin, a violation of the sixth or ninth commandment. I felt my longing took place on another plane. I felt that my desire drew on many human emotions, and so was round, perfectly round and full—hunger, weeping, joy, even a peculiar fleeting anger. The shuddering ecstasy I experienced did not produce for me the sign of a sinful act, which I always imagined as quills sprouting suddenly from my face.

Repeated readings would eventually have broken the letters' folds and marred them, so I copied each one out, word for word, and hid the copies in the ceiling of the house. I rarely went afterward to that drawer in my father's desk. When I did, I held what I called the letters of heaven so respectfully my fingers trembled. I wanted desperately to protect a quality in them I understood as purity. I could have memorized them—they were short and there were only nine—but I felt to memorize the letters would have diminished their effect. I was then, too, someone anxious about the lack of substance in memory.

In 1967, when I was eighteen, my father developed cancer. Without health insurance he knew his death was imminent, and so he soon completed the arrangements he wished to make with everyone, loving gestures that put each of us at ease. He spoke with my two uncles, the brothers with whom he ran a tannery, about the disposition of his interest there, including the skiving knives and mallets that had been his father's. He bestowed small gifts on each of his relatives. And through the generosity of his love, by the breadth of his consideration of us, he steered my mother and my sisters and myself toward a rarefied emotional position. It was as though he were tearing himself neatly out of a book while taking pains to see the page would not be missed. Even as he was dying we began to sense that we were whole without him. We would miss him very much, but he was leaving us with a grief that strengthened us.

When it came my turn to have a private moment with my father, he said without warning, "The letters, Ramón, are the most holy, the most beautiful relics in our family. You must protect them. If you have children, give them to the child who is most drawn to them. If you do not, look among your sisters' children for the one who should receive them."

At eighteen I was too old to behave like a child, even before a dying father. I could not openly and fully express the remorse and embarrassment I felt at that moment. I did not know how to beg his forgiveness. I sensed for the first time that my clandestine involvement with the letters had been a sin.

"Who wrote them?" I asked.

"Her name was Isabel, the man was called Martín."

"Were they relatives who came to Peru?"

"Yes. Isabel's brother Fernandino is your ancestor on my father's side, fourteen generations back."

I thought about that name, Fernandino, and I suddenly felt the quills pressing against the skin of my scalp. "And the man who loved her, Martín—who were his descendants? Are they living here?"

"He did not have any children," my father answered. After a moment he said, "Is this hard for you, Ramón?"

The quills were now out. I wanted to run far away until

I disappeared like an ash in the wind. "Is it Rosa de Lima?" I asked. I felt tears of fright.

"Yes," he said, reaching for my hand and holding it. "She was Rosa de Lima, he was Martín de Porres."

I was confounded. "These are the letters of saints!" I blurted.

"They are."

"But how can you—it is blasphemy, it is blasphemous!"

"No, no, Ramón, it is love. It is the love of Christ. My son, you must already know this in your soul."

"I know nothing," I shouted, pulling my hand away, "except that there is a sin here, a terrible sin." I did not want my feelings to overwhelm me, but I could feel the flush of an emotion akin to rage building inexorably with the evidence of this deception.

"There is no sin here, Ramón. I do not even believe your taking my key and making a copy was a sin. You were the person meant to have these letters."

"But what were they doing?" I yelled at him. "What were they doing?"

"Whatever was between them, all my life I have believed it was with God's blessing."

"Please excuse me, Father, but how can you speak like this on your deathbed!"

"Isn't it just now, just in this moment, Ramón, that you have changed your mind about what you have read and thought about for so many years? And yet, what has changed? Nothing. Only that another person knows. It is not the discovery of sin that is filling you with insecurity, Ramón, it is the discovery of the intimacy of real people."

I didn't know what to answer or what to confirm.

"I'm not asking you to share a knowledge of the letters with anyone, not even for you to turn back to them if you cannot bear it. My only request is that you protect them. In each generation they have had a guardian, someone to protect them from the righteous, from those who support the black-and-white distinctions of the Manichaeans, who indulge their hatred of the body. Do you understand?"

"You are saying that I must protect them from the Church?"

"Yes, but not just the Church."

I could not imagine how even to approach this task. I moved to the foot of his bed and sat in a chair.

"Ramón," he implored, "sometimes, after reading the letters, did you touch yourself?"

I could not answer.

"It was the same for me, when I was your age."

"I did not confess what happened to me as a sin," I said after a while.

"I know. I didn't either. This is what I have been trying to make clear. You must not change your feelings now because you know who wrote the letters. Do you see?"

"I will protect them," I answered. I meant it, but it was as close to speaking a lie as it is possible to come.

I burned my copies of the letters in the hour after I left my father's room. Rosa de Lima was Isabel de Flores y Oliva, the first person from the New World to be canonized. Her friend was Martín de Porres, a mulatto canonized three hundred years later. It was not the existence of their love but how to believe in its sanctity that troubled and offended me. I did not want to know how such things could be acceptable for saints.

When my father died I came into possession of the desk with the locked drawer, but I did not look at the correspondence again for more than ten years and then only to move it to another place. Occasionally I would recall a sentence, a paragraph, and it would remain with me for days.

In the summer of 1995 I was working in the library at the University of Lima, researching a paper for a scholarly journal on the early architecture of the city. After my father died, I'd gone to Italy to school, then to France and Barcelona for a while before returning to Lima. I married Camilla, whom I had known first in secondary school, and settled into a comfortable marriage with three children. The quiet domesticity of this life contrasted with my passion for work and certain ideas. I had opened a practice as an architect. My principal interests were the use of local Peruvian stone for building, the survival of Inca techniques for working the stone, and what you would have to call my curiosity about non-Euclidean physics—the development among native workmen of a kind of hybrid structural engineering that derived from alternative ideas about what holds things up. In the case of some of the older buildings in Lima, many of my concerns came together—Quechua masons had raised stone walls buttressed in perfectly sound yet wonderfully unorthodox ways.

Over the years of my professional practice I gravitated steadily toward university teaching. I found it satisfying to support the enthusiasm of younger students, and I was always glad to find one or two who were interested in the things I was interested in. During that summer of 1995 I had two such students working for me, Pedro de Ortega and Analilia Valencia. We were studying some peculiarities in seventeenth-century public buildings in Lima and Callao, when—during the course of our library research—I came upon a second set of letters between Rosa and Martín.

The moment I saw them I was certain that no one else knew what they were. Like the first letters these were unaddressed and unsigned, but the handwriting, the idiosyncrasies in punctuation and grammar, were identical. There were twenty-two of them, on the same color and texture of paper, randomly leaved in a dozen folders of unsorted material within a single box—bills of sale, ships' manifests, and public memoranda—all from the seventeenth century.

The day I discovered the letters I made a thorough search of the only other boxes of unsorted documents on the shelves to satisfy myself there were no others. By then it was after eleven in the evening. I considered concealing the letters and taking them home with me. I had not thought much about Rosa and Martín since that conversation with my father, but here I was again, acting in violation of my principles. I placed the letters in my briefcase and walked out of the library, using my authority as a professor of the university to take advantage.

When I arrived at the house Camilla was already asleep. Our youngest child, Manco, was watching television. I went directly to my study, locked the door, and read each letter carefully. The experience, carrying far into the night, shattered a carapace I had carried unacknowledged for thirty years. These letters were less explicit than the others about sexual ecstasy, but the same overwhelming testimony to the power of the physical body flew up from them. And I could now make a different sense of their meaning. These two people had grown swiftly to accept that ecstatic love was an element of spirituality, that it intensified rather than quenched the light of God. They set forth this belief so boldly it raised the hair on the back of my head.

I sat with the letters until first light, through tears that became fits of weeping, through moments of regret, of terror and resolve, reading again and again sentences in which one or the other recognized the immanence of God in the moisture of rose petals crushed between them or in a burst of wind that entwined their hair. I sat in a state of wonder at their humanity, the fearless, complete acceptance of passion. I trembled as an observer reading at the edge of this embrace, for centuries condemned. What for some couples would have been defiance was for them faith.

The emotional upheaval was an unraveling. I was swept from one corner of my beliefs to another, never remaining long in one place. I was driven on by an awakening of sexual desire, by self-pity as well as courage, by a sense of reprieve and the impulse to abandon—a spiritual revolution. The carefully maintained barrier of my emotional distance with Camilla and others and the strict dichotomies around which my judgments occurred daily without reflection had shrunk by dawn to irrelevancy.

I knew enough of the lives of Rosa and Martín, remembered mostly from the popular but improbable hagiographies of my childhood, to understand how the relationship revealed in their letters might have come about and to accept the plausibility of everything set out in them. Martín was born in 1579, Rosa seven years later. She lived in a house with ten brothers and sisters on Calle de Santo Domingo, adjacent to the Dominican monastery Martín entered as a lay helper when he was fifteen. Rosa's mother, Maria de Flores, was an irritable, hot-tempered woman. Her father, who participated as a professional soldier in the defeat of the Pizarros at Jaquijahuana, later became superintendent of the silver mines at Quives. Rosa helped support the family by selling flowers she raised in a garden that shared a wall with the monastery gardens Martín de Porres attended.

Rosa was canonized in 1671. Sainthood for Martín did not come until 1962—a delay caused, some say, by the fact that he was dark-skinned. The transcribed testimony of their contemporaries, provided to apostolic tribunals convened at the time of each one's death, is explicit and almost without contradiction concerning the holiness of each person. The extent of their charity toward the destitute, the injured, the abandoned, was then and remains for us now unfathomable. The infusion of physical comfort and spiritual solace each conveyed to ease every kind of human suffering was so inexplicable, so unearthly, it must be regarded as miraculous. A striking sign of their blessedness is that both Rosa and Martín were repeatedly discovered elevated three or four feet off the ground before the Crucifix in a state of spiritual ecstasy or oblivion.

At the time of their ministries, life for many in Lima was an unmitigated horror. The city teemed with gangs of orphans. Epidemic disease was rampant. The many victims of the depraved and bloody administration of the Spanish viceroyalty lived crowded in hovels throughout the city and swarmed the streets for the garbage and waste on which they survived. Reading records of that time, one is soon confirmed in the belief that this was a period of human derangement—the whipping of Church-owned slaves, the public rape of street urchins. It was into this debilitating and sordid atmosphere that Rosa and Martín were born and in which each developed a sense of God.

Of the two, Rosa was the more reclusive. At the age of thirteen she came to believe adamantly that only by devoting herself to prayer, to the most abject supplication before God, might she find salvation. She cut herself off from human society, embarked on a period of harsh fasts, and regularly beat herself with sticks. Her many chroniclers are at pains to describe her self-flagellation as "masochistic and abnormal," but looking at the letters and the entirety of her life, I believe her behavior was instead an act of rage against the darkness manifest in the streets around her and which she also saw in herself. Her biographers refer to these seven years as her "period of aridity." It was near the end of this time that she met Martín.

The Dominican friar was much more outgoing, a humorous, energetic man, the son of an hidalgo named Juan de Porres and of Anna Velasquez, a Panamanian woman variously described as an Indian and as a free black. Martín lived the impoverished life of a religious abject but was so enthusiastic about human life and so ready with self-deprecating jokes that he confounded those who piously recorded his miraculous cures of the terminally ill. Each day he walked out into the streets of Lima to help whomever he met. Like Rosa, who turned her parents' home into a hospice for abused prostitutes, Martín brought the most deracinated and wretched back to the monastery, housing them in his own small cell if necessary. His charity was celebrated throughout Lima; the wealthy sought his counsel and showered him with money.

During the months in which the letters were written, in the fall of 1606, I think, Rosa was twenty. She was just entering a period of serenity in her life, a time of transcendent beatitude such as people often imagine to be the equanimity of angels. It lasted until she died in 1617, at the age of thirty-one. Martín would have been twenty-seven in 1606. Among his official duties at the monastery were his responsibilities in the hospital and in the garden, but he spent much of his time in the streets. In a city blighted by ambitious schemes and cruel enforcements, he was for all the pariahs an elevating hand, a sympathetic ear.

Rosa and Martín, lacking a certain cupidity and the designs of power that would have drawn them more completely into the world, nevertheless willingly engaged in its terrors. Against holiness like theirs one has no recourse, no protection. It was part of the reason I broke down that night.

I slept most of the day after my night of reading and catharsis. The following day Camilla and Manco went to Callao to visit his grandmother, and I had the house to myself. I took out the nine letters my father had given me and read them for the first time in many years. I had then a sudden, intuitive sense of the order of all the letters. Assembled along these lines they revealed a clear evolution of psychological and spiritual ideas.

The letters my father gave me seem all to have been among the earliest written. Their composers describe with wonder and joy each other's smallest physical attributes. They dwell on the blinding ecstasy produced by mere touch—the inside of the wrist, say, lifting the bare flesh of the breast. Rosa writes of the heat and the pressure she experiences straining against him, the sensation of his penetration she feels in her spine, the delirious loss of her mind. Martín writes of the inexplicable tears that wet their faces, the thrill of restraint and hesitation in his tongue drawn across the shuddering currents of her skin. They make love in her garden most often. In their letters they speculate at the way they tear plants from the ground in their ravishment and at her compulsion to ride him like a horse, and they recall how in a kiss Martín had unfurled honey against her teeth and then slowly caressed every part of her mouth he could reach.

In those early letters they seem to affirm not physical passion so much as entry upon a form of reverie both familiar and unknown to them, a capacity for such experience that for them must have been an abiding hunger. In subsequent letters (the majority of these from the library) they explore the meaning of this elevated state, and they consider the unity they have discovered through it—with each other, with jasmine blossoms that fall on them in the garden, and with their spiritual calling, the prayer and ministration that shaped the hours of their daily lives.

It's my feeling that I have read most of the letters they wrote, that there were few earlier or later ones. The letters originate in the realm of physical sensation, move to a more ethereal realm (though still rooted in the physical), and culminate in what appears to be the completion of an understanding of what they were striving for. I would guess that all of the letters were written during a period of only two or three months, and I see the evidence of this intense companionship most clearly in a change in Rosa's life. Certain references in the letters suggest that Martín prevailed upon Rosa to cease beating herself. Rosa had as profound an effect, I think, on Martín's life, though this is harder to discern. If Rosa's "period of aridity" came to an end during these months, this, too, was possibly the time that Martín acquired the gift that permitted him to speak to animals. Before this, his love had embraced even the most wounded human being; following upon his intimacy with Rosa, the tenderness he exhibited was undiscriminating and unbounded. It extended toward all life.

In what I feel was the final letter, Rosa tells Martín that as a sign of their love, of the "elimination of the barriers that exclude God," they should regularly place vases of flowers on the garden wall, where the arrangements would be visible to each of them. Indeed, in statements included in testimony taken down by the apostolic tribunals, I've found references to the fact that until their last day it was the habit of each of these people to place bouquets of flowers on their common wall, the instances of this noted because no matter what the season, vivid displays of lilies and roses appeared.

The letters of Rosa and Martín have compelled my salvation, but they have also created a dilemma for me. My foremost responsibility, I believe, is to protect them from fanatics, from obliteration or derision. (Curious, how late in life has come the realization of what my father meant.) In the days following my discovery of the letters in the library, however, I developed such an affection toward the world, such a sense of tenderness toward anyone caught in the predicament of life, that I came to view publication of the letters as an urgent matter. By means of this one gesture, I thought, so much of the putrefaction and hypocrisy of evil could be wiped away. I now saw the physical attraction between my students, Pedro and Analilia, not as mundane carnality but as unperfected desire, and within that a potential for pervading love, whether or not they decided to marry. With Camilla, whom I had become so remote from, who had become almost an idea to me, I rediscovered simple sensual pleasure. Perhaps most striking for me was the recovery of a sense of the vastness of the world outside my own concerns and aspirations.

What would seem astonishing to a modern reader of these letters, of course, is that two saints embraced the physical hunger that enveloped them instead of running from it. They took it as a sign of God. Then, riding a wave of passion large enough to drown most of us, they transmuted that clutching, compressing, exhausting physical love into a deeper knowledge of God, achieving a peace in their own lives that they gave away in all the dark corners of Lima.

Even as I saw the good that could come from publishing the letters, however, I knew it was being realistic rather than cynical to see that any such publication in Peru would be suppressed, or so thoroughly undermined that the letters would finally be dismissed as forgeries. The Church would call it blasphemy, Hollywood would beat at the door with money and offer solemn promises. The endurance of these letters through fourteen generations would then culminate in an explosion. They would fall back to the earth like so much confetti.

By some means, however, I intend to release these letters. It is amazing that love like this is the experience of saints, but the apparatus of sainthood and Catholicism, it seems to me, is not essential in the story of these people, only knowledge of the spiritual life to be found at the core of their physical experience. Ecstasy seems directionless to me, but like all passion, it might be directed toward the divine.

I am considering several courses of action. If I forward copies of the letters to a friend in China, a scholar of religion at the University of Wuhan, he could arrange for their publication there. They would then emerge as a kind of heresy and so enjoy that protection. I am also considering paying for their publication in Lima under the auspices of a spurious monastery in Catalonia. Eventually they would be discredited by the Church as a work of fiction, but they would suffer less that way than if the authorities were forced to treat them as a reality.

The letters, of course, have given me my first understanding of the humanity of saints. I've written out passages from them on small slips of paper which I meditate upon during Mass. For example, in one letter Martín describes how he wishes to place his lips in a depression above Rosa's clavicle and draw from it the poisonous residue left by her father's beatings, which she had endured as a child. In another letter Rosa speaks of the power of memory to kindle desire when presented with a certain scene—the undulating flight of swallows reminds her of the swoon of physical ecstasy, the overlapping songs of finches in the garden at dawn restore the sensation of his first touch.

For now, I will keep the letters I took from the library. I don't know how to resolve the theft, but it can wait until I see a way through this larger responsibility. I've never discussed the letters with Camilla. I have not discussed them with my eldest son, Artaud, though I am actually inclined to pass them on to our middle child, Elouisa. She has a quick, irreverent mind, but she is the most principled person in the family and contains, I suspect, the deepest waters. I consider that it has fallen to me only to have made this additional discovery in the university library, to complete the collection of letters. Now that their meaning is so clear, it may be for Elouisa to determine our next step.

When Camilla and I were courting, I took images from the letters to astonish and impress her. I now believe this the only sin, the one failure of integrity that I persisted in with these letters. It filled me with such shame that I later confessed the sin many times, to be forgiven again and again.

One evening I will ask Camilla to go for a walk with me. I hope to direct us to some place along the Río Rímac, a spot where the other two might once have stood.

RESTORATION

Just over the Montana border in North Dakota, north of the small town of Killdeer, there is a French mansion. It is part of a frontier estate built in 1863 for a titled family called de Crenir, from Bordeaux. When the last of the de Crenirs died in France in 1904, the two-story Victorian house, its contents, and the surrounding acres were bequeathed to the nearby town. Looking incongruous still in the vast landscape of brown hills, it has since stood as a tourist attraction.

There are various explanations for why the house was built in such a desolate place, after the fur trade had passed on but before the Indian wars were over and settlement had come. In time, the Great Northern Railroad reached it, but the first de Crenirs had to come up by boat seven hundred miles from St. Louis and finish the journey by horse. According to a pamphlet given to tourists, the family had had thoughts of establishing a cattle empire, but their visits were irregular and short. In spite of the rich furnishings freighted in and installed and the considerable expense and trouble involved in construction, only one, René de Crenir, ever overwintered there. His visits began in the spring of 1883 and he arrived each spring thereafter, departing each fall until he took up permanent residence in 1887. Seven years later, in the summer of 1894, he left abruptly, and no de Crenir ever came again. This young de Crenir, too, the pamphlet goes on to say, was the only one of the family to visit regularly with people in town, or who rode more than a day's journey into the surrounding country.

The gray and white house gives the impression now of being a military outpost on the edge of an empire of silence and space, the domain, at the time it was built, of buffalo, bear, antelope, wolves, Hunkpapa Sioux, Crows off to the west, and others. Today there is little of value left beyond the house itself and a few pieces of period furniture except a collection of extraordinary books.

In the summer of 1974, this collection was in the process of being restored by a man named Edward Seraut. I was driving east and saw a highway advertisement outside Killdeer—HISTORIC FRENCH CHATEAU • 12 MILES • ICE CREAM • COOL DRINKS • SOUVENIRS—and had stopped and toured the mansion with other people on vacation. Afterward, with a guard's permission and anticipating a conversation, I went back to the library on the second floor and introduced myself, somewhat hesitantly, to Seraut.

I had been struck right away by the sight of him, sitting still and jacketless in a straight chair with a broken book in his lap, as though bereaved. He was perhaps in his sixties. He seemed gratified by my interest, though I startled him when I came up. He showed me, still with a slightly quizzical look, a few of the books he had been working on—an oversized folio of colored prints of North American mammals by Karl Bodmer, and a copy, I recognized, of La Mettrie's *L'Homme Machine*. He described a technique he was just then using to remove a stain called foxing from a flyleaf. I was drawn to him. When I asked if I might take him to dinner, he said he would be glad—delighted.

"I've been here for months," he said, "and I've hardly looked out the windows."

While I waited for the estate to close—Seraut said he was obliged to work in public view until closing time—I walked out into the surrounding hills. They had a smoothness of line, an evenness of tone, that is often called graceful, the sun-dried grasses being everywhere the same height. I wondered if these might be the native grasses, come back. The dry hills seemed without life, though in the distance, through shimmering heat waves, some Herefords or other kind of cattle were grazing.

When I returned to the house, Seraut was not quite ready and, glad to watch, I insisted he go on. His tools appeared surgical. Laid out on a long refectory table, amid presses and rolls of paper and leather, were forceps and scalpels, tweezers, syringes filled with glue, many spools of thread and several kinds of knives. The room was filled, too, with a pleasing light, but when I remarked about it, Seraut said this was one of the reasons the collection had deteriorated—that, and the fact that many of the books had been so heavily used. He indicated the worn headband on a book as he handed it to me. I knew this book, too, William Bartram's *Travels Through North and South Carolina*— a first edition. But I was mesmerized more by Seraut's efficiency. He had beveled a frayed corner clean and then anchored a new piece of book board to it with tiny steel pins, like a bone fracture. When he covered the corner with leather, the matching of line and texture was so deft the repair seemed never to have been made. Indeed, like the other corners, it appeared slightly rubbed from use.

He firmed the book in a small press and we left.

On the way into town we both marveled at the broad reach, the sultry reds and oranges, the lingering yellows, of the North Dakota sunset. Seraut remarked on the fine shading of colors, their densities. Leathers, he said, after a moment, could be treated with certain vegetable dyes to achieve a range of color as subtle. I asked, did one, in taking advantage of such skills, restore a book so well it avoided detection? Or did one leave clear evidence of what had been done, so as not to confuse the issue of originality? He leaned toward the former, he said, but always tipped a small sheet of paper into the back of the book, noting the date of restoration and what he had done.

I had been attracted to Seraut because of his work, and the atmosphere of well-read books; but there was a kind of incongruity about him, too, that was as attractive. His dress was foreign, a dark wool suit, a white shirt with a plain dark tie. He was mannered—a suggestion of polite intentions and cultivated tastes. There was almost the air of a prior about him. He seemed oblivious to the country in which he was now at work.

He had been hired, he told me, by a man in Illinois, a lawyer who had bought the de Crenir collection. A committee of townspeople had advertised it for sale in order to raise money to refurbish the mansion—629 leather-bound volumes belonging to René de Crenir, most on topics of natural history, some dating from the sixteenth century. The man had asked Seraut to travel to North Dakota, to restore the collection and prepare it for shipment east.

Seraut said he spent his days filling insect holes, repairing deteriorating spines, restoring gold tooling—"accurate and sympathetic restoration," he told me, "not crude mutilations or the inappropriate embellishments of amateurs." If necessary he would dismantle a book entirely in order to resize and rehinge each page, before sewing it all back together. He had been working for three months but would need another few weeks, he thought, to finish. He lived at the de Crenir mansion. He said nothing of any contact with the townspeople. The afternoon I met him he had paid no attention at all to the tourists who had wandered through.

Over dinner, perhaps because of the wine, he spoke with sudden passion of the art and obscurity of his profession, at one point emphasizing the obscurity with a gesture of his arm toward the far reaches of the prairie that lay beyond the walls of the hotel. I tried to listen politely but was caught by an offhand reference to being able to reconstruct René de Crenir's intellectual life, through a study of the collection. How? I asked.

The volumes that have seen the most use, he went on, indicated de Crenir's principal concern was with the presence of animals in North America that were unknown in Europe. The library contained first editions of the journals and letters of James Oglethorpe, Thomas Nuttall, André

Michaux, and Cadwallader Colden, all of whom were among the earliest to make extensive, first-hand notes on the natural history of North America. There were copies, too, of many of the early accounts of plains exploration— Lewis and Clark, Bradbury, Stewart. Seraut said he believed de Crenir had been *obsessed* with understanding the nature of animals foreign to the European mind, that he wanted a *new* understanding, rooted in North America and representing a radically different view of the place of animals in human ideas.

To want to try to do this, I said, was certainly reasonable. European naturalists had groped at first for European analogs to describe unfamiliar animals—they had referred to American coyotes, for example, as jackals. The stories of alligators and eight-foot diamondback rattlesnakes they brought home were not taken seriously, nor was the idea that a grizzly bear might not be fazed by three or four bullets. The soulless vision of creatures set forth at the time by Descartes and Linnaeus was not affected by the North American discoveries and it soon absorbed them, passing right over the native taxonomies. De Crenir, I said, may have wanted to throw out the European system and fit the American animals to a new system—but how?

We ordered brandy and cigars after dinner. I was now deeply affected by the atmosphere of ideas and history that emanated from Seraut, and periodically stunned by the sight of young, ferine men cruising in slow-moving pickups on the other side of the window, or distracted by the rise and fall of ranchers' voices and the din of country-and-western music in an adjoining bar. As Seraut speculated, I became more and more fascinated by de Crenir.

Had he ever published? Seraut shrugged. Perhaps, but he thought not. There were only stray notes, no manuscripts. Risking the feeling of camaraderie, I asked if I could examine the library the next day. I knew some natural history; perhaps I could construct an outline of de Crenir's work. Seraut said he had no objection, though I sensed he thought my interest precipitate and improper.

I drove him back. In the August moonlight, the North Dakota hills appeared in soft outline, gentle and unearthly.

By the time I arrived the next morning the first visitors had already been through. Seraut was at work in shirt sleeves. Not wishing to disturb him, I began to read the titles of books on the shelves, examining a few at random as I went along. One I pulled down, on the classification of European butterflies, was interspersed with thin sheets of paper on which were written notes in French—I assumed in René de Crenir's hand—about Hermes, Atalanta, and others from Greek mythology. Similar notes in other books referred to the Eddas, the Bhagavad Gita. Those books not concerned with natural history bore mostly on religion, philosophy, and Catholic theology.

Underneath a pair of tall casement windows there was an empty table. With an enquiring nod to Seraut, who looked up expressionless from what he was doing, I laid out several volumes and began to make notes of my own. I worked through a long morning, looking away occasionally only to study the older man. His fingers were crooked slightly with arthritis but moved deliberately and adroitly over his materials. In the bright sunlight slanting into the high-ceilinged room the thin skin of his forearms appeared glassine. He seemed, even in this library, an anachronism.

From what I could discover, de Crenir was an anti-rationalist, at odds with the Age of Reason, a champion of Montaigne. Once or twice I engaged Seraut in conversation, briefly sharing my ideas and enthusiasm. He directed me to other volumes; though he was taken up with its restoration, his interest in the contents of the collection seemed as intent. From these titles, their chapters and marginal notes, I gleaned that de Crenir believed a cultural and philosophic bias had prevented nineteenth-century European naturalists from comprehending much of the plant and animal life they saw in North America. The resulting confusion, he believed, had kept them in ignorance of something even more profound: de Crenir had written in the margin of Maximilian's *Reise in das innere Nord-Amerika,* "Ici les bêtes sont les propriétaires"—in North America the indigenous philosophy grew out of the lives of animals.

De Crenir was largely correct—as subsequent work by anthropologists made clear. What was so startling was that in the whole of his library there were only eight or ten books that bore in any way at all on native American philosophy, only such things as the works of James Hall. De Crenir had apparently reached these conclusions alone.

From here, I did not know where to go. If de Crenir thought animals the owners of the landscape, or even, in theological terms, equal with men, whom might he have spoken with about it? Whom had he written?

———

Mr. Seraut and I had a late lunch together by one of the large windows. He seemed pleased by my findings. I said, out of a rush of ideas, that I might work on here for several days if that was all right and then possibly contact a friend who spoke excellent French. He showed me a book he had just taken out of the press. When I hesitated to hold it because of its beauty, he urged me to take it, to listen to the rattle of its pages, to examine the retooling. When he took the book back he said he preferred the older traditions. Where gold tooling was now restored with the aid of shellacs, he still used egg whites and vinegar, as had been done for four hundred years. His glues were still made from wheat flour. They would outlast the paper in some of the books.

I asked him over our sandwiches if he had ever read any of Montaigne. Oh yes. Once, in Leningrad, he had restored a bound collection of Montaigne's letters. He had read Montaigne's misgivings about his work in his own hand. He spoke in a genial way, as though misgivings were a part of everything.

Out the window we could see several miles across the rolling brown hills. In a draw below the house there suddenly appeared six antelope, frozen so still they seemed to shimmer in the dry grass. I saw sunlight glinting on the surface of their huge eyes, their hearts beating against soft, cream-white throats, the slender legs. Surprised by the house, or by us in the window, they were as suddenly gone. At the end of the room, beyond a blue velvet rope strung between polished brass stanchions, a line of tourists passed. They stared at us and then looked away nervously into the shelves of books. A girl in yellow shorts was eating ice cream. In a shaft of window light I could see the wheat paste dried to granules under Seraut's fingernails and the excessive neatness of my own notes, the black ink like a skittering of shore birds over the white sheets.

THE MAPPIST

When I was an undergraduate at Brown I came across a book called *The City of Ascensions,* about Bogotá. I knew nothing of Bogotá, but I felt the author had captured its essence. My view was that Onesimo Peña had not written a travel book but a work about the soul of Bogotá. Even if I were to read it later in life, I thought, I would not be able to get all Peña meant in a single reading. I looked him up at the library but he had apparently written no other books, at least not any in English.

In my senior year I discovered a somewhat better known book, *The City of Trembling Leaves,* by Walter Van Tilburg Clark, about Reno, Nevada. I liked it, but it did not have the superior depth, the integration of Peña's work. Peña, you had the feeling, could walk you through the warrens of Bogotá without a map and put your hands directly on the vitality of any modern century—the baptismal registries of a particular cathedral, a cornerstone that had been taken from one building to be used in another, a London plane tree planted by Bolívar. He had such a command of the idiom of this city, and the book itself demonstrated such complex linkages, it was easy to believe Peña had no other subject, that he could have written nothing else. I believed this was so until I read *The City of Floating Sand* a year later, a book about Cape Town, and then a book about Djakarta, called *The City of Frangipani*. Though the former was by one Frans Haartman and the latter by a Jemboa Tran, each had the distinctive organic layering of the Peña book, and I felt certain they'd been written by the same man.

A national library search through the University of Michigan, where I had gone to work on a master's degree in geography, produced hundreds of books with titles similar to these. I had to know whether Peña had written any others and so read or skimmed perhaps thirty of those I got through interlibrary loan. Some, though wretched, were strange enough to be engaging; others were brilliant but not in the way of Peña. I ended up ordering copies of five I believed Peña had written, books about Perth, Lagos, Tokyo, Venice, and Boston, the last a volume by William Smith Everett called *The City of Cod*.

Who Peña actually was I could not then determine. Letters to publishers eventually led me to a literary agency in New York where I was told that the author did not wish to be known. I pressed for information about what else he might have written, inquired whether he was still alive (the book about Venice had been published more than fifty years before), but got nowhere.

As a doctoral student at Duke I made the seven Peña books the basis of a dissertation. I wanted to show in a series of city maps, based on all the detail in Peña's descriptions, what a brilliant exegesis of the social dynamics of these cities he had achieved. My maps showed, for example, how water moved through Djakarta, not just municipal water but also trucked water and, street by street, the flow of rainwater. And how road building in Cape Town reflected the policy of apartheid.

I received quite a few compliments on the work, but I knew the maps did not make apparent the hard, translucent jewel of integration that was each Peña book. I had only created some illustrations, however well done. But had I known whether he was alive or where he lived, I would still have sent him a copy out of a sense of collegiality and respect.

After I finished the dissertation I moved my wife and three young children to Brookline, a suburb of Boston, and set up a practice as a restoration geographer. Fifteen years later I embarked on my fourth or fifth trip to Tokyo as a consultant to a planning firm there, and one evening I took a train out to Chiyoda-ku to visit bookstores in an area called Jimbocho. Just down the street from a bridge over the Kanda River is the Sanseido Book Store, a regular haunt by then for me. Up on the fifth floor I bought two translations of books by Japanese writers on the Asian architectural response to topography in mountain cities. I was exiting the store on the ground floor, a level given over entirely to maps, closing my coat against the spring night, when I happened to spot the kanji for "Tokyo" on a tier of drawers. I opened one of them to browse. Toward the bottom of a second drawer, I came upon a set of maps that seemed vaguely familiar, though the entries were all in kanji. After a few minutes of leafing through, it dawned on me that they bore a resemblance to the maps I had done as a student at Duke. I was considering buying one of them as a memento when I caught a name in English in the corner—Corlis Benefideo. It appeared there on every map.

I stared at that name a long while, and I began to consider what you also may be thinking. I bought all thirteen maps. Even without language to identify information in the keys, even without titles, I could decipher what the mapmaker was up to. One designated areas prone to flooding as water from the Sumida River backed up through the city's storm drains. Another showed the location of all shops dealing in Edo Period manuscripts and artwork. Another, using small pink arrows, showed the point of view of each of Hiroshige's famous One Hundred Views. Yet another showed, in six time-sequenced panels, the rise and decline of horse barns in the city.

My office in Boston was fourteen hours behind me, so I had to leave a message for my assistant, asking him to look up Corlis Benefideo's name. I gave him some contacts at map libraries I used regularly, and asked him to call me back as soon as he had anything, no matter the hour. He called at three a.m. to say that Corlis Benefideo had worked as a mapmaker for the U.S. Coast and Geodetic Survey in Washington from 1932 until 1958, and that he was going to fax me some more information.

I dressed and went down to the hotel lobby to wait for the faxes and read them while I stood there. Benefideo was born in Fargo, North Dakota, in 1912. He went to work for the federal government straight out of Grinnell College during the Depression and by 1940 was traveling to various places—Venice, Bogotá, Lagos—in an exchange program. In 1958 he went into private practice as a cartographer in Chicago. His main source of income at that time appeared to be from the production of individualized site maps for large estate homes being built along the North Shore of Lake Michigan. The maps were bound in oversize books, twenty by thirty inches, and showed the vegetation, geology, hydrology, biology, and even archaeology of each site. They were subcontracted for under several architects.

Benefideo's Chicago practice closed in 1975. The fax said nothing more was known of his work history, and that he was not listed in any Chicago area phone books, nor with any professional organizations. I faxed back to my office, asking them to check phone books in Fargo, in Washington, D.C., and around Grinnell, Iowa—Des Moines and those towns. And asking them to try to find someone at what was now the National Geodetic Survey who might have known Benefideo or who could provide some detail.

When I came back to the hotel the following afternoon, there was another fax. No luck with the phone books, I read, but I could call a Maxwell Abert at the National Survey who'd worked with Benefideo. I waited the necessary few hours for the time change and called.

Abert said he had overlapped with Benefideo for one year, 1958, and though Benefideo had left voluntarily, it wasn't his idea.

"What you had to understand about Corlis," he said, "was that he was a patriot. Now, that word today, I don't know, means maybe nothing, but Corlis felt this very strong commitment to his country, and to a certain kind of mapmaking, and he and the Survey just ended up on a collision course. The way Corlis worked, you see, the way he approached things, slowed down the production of maps. That wasn't any good from a bureaucratic point of view. He couldn't give up being comprehensive, you understand, and they just didn't know what to do with him."

"What happened to him?"

"Well, the man spoke five or six languages, and he had both the drafting ability and the conceptual skill of a first-rate cartographer, so the government should have done something to keep the guy—and he was also very loyal—but they didn't. Oh, his last year they created a project for him, but it was temporary. He saw they didn't want him. He moved to Chicago—but you said you knew that."

"Mmm. Do you know where he went after Chicago?"

"I do. He went to Fargo. And that's the last I know. I wrote him there until about 1985—he'd have been in his seventies—and then the last letter came back 'no forwarding address.' So that's the last I heard. I believe he must have died. He'd be, what, eighty-eight now."

"What was the special project?"

"Well Corlis, you know, he was like something out of a WPA project, like Dorothea Lange, Walker Evans and James Agee and them, people that had this sense of America as a country under siege, undergoing a trial during the Depression, a society that needed its dignity back. Corlis believed that in order to effect any political or social change, you had to know exactly what you were talking about. You had to know what the country itself—the ground, the real thing, not some political abstraction—was all about. So he proposed this series of forty-eight sets of maps—this was just before Alaska and Hawaii came in—a series for each state that would show the geology and hydrology, where the water was, you know, and the botany and biology, and the history of the place from Native American times.

"Well, a hundred people working hundred-hour weeks for a decade might get it all down, you know—it was monumental, what he was proposing. But to keep him around, to have him in the office, the Survey created this pilot project so he could come up with an approach that might get it done in a reasonable amount of time—why, I don't know; the government works on most things for-ever—but that's what he did. I never saw the results, but if you ever wanted to see disillusionment in a man, you should have seen Corlis in those last months. He tried congressmen, he tried senators, he tried other people in Commerce, he tried everybody, but I think they all had the same sense of him, that he was an obstructionist. They'd eat a guy like that alive on the Hill today, the same way. He just wasn't very practical. But he was a good man."

I got the address in Fargo and thanked Mr. Abert. It turned out to be where Benefideo's parents had lived until they died. The house was sold in 1985. And that was that.

When I returned to Boston I reread *The City of Ascensions*. It's a beautiful book, so tender toward the city, and pro-ceeding on the assumption the Bogotá was the living idea of its inhabitants. I thought Benefideo's books would make an exceptional subject for a senior project in history or geography, and wanted to suggest it to my older daughter,

Stephanie. How, I might ask her, do we cultivate people like Corlis Benefideo? Do they all finally return to the rural districts from which they come, unable or unwilling to fully adapt to the goals, the tone, of a progressive society? Was Corlis familiar with the work of Lewis Mumford? Would you call him a populist?

Stephanie, about to finish her junior year at Bryn Mawr, had an interest in cities and geography, but I didn't know how to follow up on this with her. Her interests were there in spite of my promotions.

One morning, several months after I got back from Tokyo, I walked into the office and saw a note in the center of my desk, a few words from my diligent assistant. It was Benefideo's address—Box 117, Garrison, North Dakota 58540. I got out the office atlas. Garrison is halfway between Minot and Bismarck, just north of Lake Sakakawea. No phone.

I wrote him a brief letter, saying I'd recently bought a set of his maps in Tokyo, asking if he was indeed the author of the books, and telling him how much I admired them and that I had based my Ph.D. dissertation on them. I praised the integrity of the work he had done, and said I was intrigued by his last Survey project, and would also like to see one of the Chicago publications sometime.

A week later I got a note. "Dear Mr. Trevino," it read.

I appreciate your kind words about my work. I am still at it. Come for a visit if you wish. I will be back from a trip in late September, so the first week of October would be fine. Sincerely, Corlis Benefideo.

I located a motel in Garrison, got plane tickets to Bismarck, arranged a rental car, and then wrote Mr. Benefideo and told him I was coming, and that if he would send me his street address I would be at his door at nine a.m. on October second. The address he sent, 15088 State Highway 37, was a few miles east of Garrison. A hand-rendered map in colored pencil, which made tears well up in my eyes, showed how to get to the house, which lay a ways off the road in a grove of ash trees he had sketched.

The days of waiting made me anxious and aware of my vulnerability. I asked both my daughters and my son if they wanted to go. No, school was starting, they wanted to be with their friends. My wife debated, then said no. She thought this was something that would go best if I went alone.

Corlis was straddling the sill of his door as I drove in to his yard. He wore a pair of khaki trousers, a khaki shirt, and a khaki ball cap. He was about five foot six and lean. Though spry, he showed evidence of arthritis and the other infirmities of age in his walk and handshake.

During breakfast I noticed a set of *The City of* books on his shelves. There were eight, which meant I'd missed one. After breakfast he asked if I'd brought any binoculars, and whether I'd be interested in visiting a wildlife refuge a few miles away off the Bismarck highway, to watch ducks and geese coming in from Canada. He made a picnic lunch and we drove over and had a fine time. I had no binoculars with me, and little interest in the birds to start with, but with his guidance and animation I came to appreciate the place. We saw more than a million birds that day, he said.

When we got back to the house I asked if I could scan his bookshelves while he fixed dinner. He had thousands of books, a significant number of them in Spanish and French and some in Japanese. (The eighth book was called *The City of Geraniums,* about Lima.) On the walls of a large room that incorporated the kitchen and dining area was perhaps the most astonishing collection of hand-drawn maps I had ever seen outside a library. Among them were two of McKenzie's map sketches from his exploration of northern Canada; four of FitzRoy's coastal elevations from Chile, made during the voyage with Darwin; one of Humboldt's maps of the Orinoco; and a half dozen sketches of the Thames docks by Samuel Pepys.

Mr. Benefideo made us a dinner of canned soup, canned meat, and canned vegetables. For dessert he served fresh fruit, some store-bought cookies, and instant coffee. I studied him at the table. His forehead was high, and a prominent jaw and large nose further elongated his face. His eyes were pale blue, his skin burnished and dark, like a Palermo fisherman's. His ears flared slightly. His hair, still black on top, was close-cropped. There was little in the face but the alertness of the eyes to give you a sense of the importance of his work.

After dinner our conversation took a more satisfying turn. He had discouraged conversation while we were watching the birds, and he had seemed disinclined to talk while he was riding in the car. Our exchanges around dinner—which was quick—were broken up by its preparation and by clearing the table. A little to my surprise, he offered me Mexican tequila after the meal. I declined, noticing the bottle had no label, but sat with him on the porch while he drank.

Yes, he said, he'd used the pen names to keep the government from finding out what else he'd been up to in those cities. And yes, the experiences with the Survey had made him a little bitter, but it had also opened the way to other things. His work in Chicago had satisfied him—the map sets for the estate architects and their wealthy clients, he made clear, were a minor thing; his real business in those years was in other countries, where hand-drawn and hand-colored maps still were welcome and enthused over. The estate map books, however, had allowed him to keep his hand in on the kind of work he wanted to pursue more fully one day. In 1975 he came back to Fargo to take care of his parents. When they died he sold the house and moved to Garrison. He had a government pension—when he said this he flicked his eyebrows, as though in the end he had gotten the best of the government. He had a small income from his books, he told me, mostly the foreign editions. And he had put some money away, so he'd been able to buy this place.

"What are you doing now?"

"The North Dakota series, the work I proposed in Washington in fifty-seven."

"The hydrological maps, the biological maps?"

"Yes. I subdivided the state into different sections, the actual number depending on whatever scale I needed for that subject. I've been doing them for fifteen years now, a thousand six hundred and fifty-one maps. I want to finish them, you know, so that if anyone ever wants to duplicate the work, they'll have a good idea of how to go about it."

He gazed at me in a slightly disturbing, almost accusatory way.

"Are you going to donate the maps, then, to a place where they can be studied?"

"North Dakota Museum of Art, in Grand Fork."

"Did you never marry, never have children?"

"I'm not sure, you know. No, I never married—I asked a few times, but was turned down. I didn't have the features, I think, and, early on, no money. Afterward, I developed a way of life that was really too much my own on a day-to-day basis. But, you know, I've been the beneficiary of great kindness in my life, and some of it has come from women who were, or are, very dear to me. Do you know what I mean?"

"Yes, I do."

"As for children, I think maybe there are one or two. In Bogotá. Venice. Does it shock you?"

"People are not shocked by things like this anymore, Mister Benefideo."

"That's too bad. I am. I have made my peace with it, though. Would you like to see the maps?"

"The Dakota series?"

Mr. Benefideo took me to a second large room with more stunning maps on the walls, six or eight tiers of large map drawers, and a worktable the perimeter of which was stained with hundreds of shades of watercolors surrounding a gleaming white area about three feet square. He turned on some track lighting which made the room very bright and pointed me to a swivel stool in front of an empty table, a smooth, broad surface of some waxed and dark wood.

From an adjacent drawer he pulled out a set of large maps, which he laid in front of me.

"As you go through, swing them to the side there. I'll restack them."

The first map was of ephemeral streams in the northeast quadrant of the state.

"These streams," he pointed out, "run only during wet periods, some but once in twenty years. Some don't have any names."

The information was strikingly presented and beautifully drawn. The instruction you needed to get oriented— where the Red River was, where the county lines were— was just enough, so it barely impinged on the actual subject matter of the map. The balance was perfect.

The next map showed fence lines, along the Missouri River in a central part of the state.

"These are done at twenty-year intervals, going back to eighteen forty. Fences are like roads, they proliferate. They're never completely removed."

The following map was a geological rendering of McIntosh County's bedrock geology. As I took in the shape and colors, the subdivided shades of purple and green and blue, Mr. Benefideo slid a large hand-colored transparency across the sheet, a soil map of the same area. You could imagine looking down through a variety of soil types to the bedrock below.

"Or," he said, and slid an opaque map with the same information across in front of me, the yellows and browns of a dozen silts, clays, and sands.

The next sheet was of eighteenth- and nineteenth-century foot trails in the western half of the state.

"But how did you compile this information?"

"Inspection and interviews. Close personal observation and talking with long-term residents. It's a hard thing, really, to erase a trail. A lot of information can be recovered if you stay at it."

When he placed the next map in front of me, the summer distribution of Swainson's hawks, and then slid in next to it a map showing the overlapping summer distribution of its main prey species, the Richardson ground squirrel, the precision and revelation were too much for me.

I turned to face him. "I've never seen anything that even approaches this, this"—my gesture across the surface of the table included everything. "It's not just the information, or the execution—I mean, the technique is flawless, the watercoloring, your choice of scale—but it's like the books, there's so much more."

"That's the idea, don't you think, Mister Trevino?"

"Of course, but nobody has the time for this kind of fieldwork anymore."

"That's unfortunate, because this information is what we need, you know. This shows history and how people fit the places they occupy. It's about what gets erased and what comes to replace it. These maps reveal the foundations beneath the ephemera."

"What about us, though?" I blurted, resisting his pronouncement. "In the books, in *City in Aspic* in particular, there is such a palpable love of human life in the cities, and here—"

"I do not have to live up to the history of Venice, Mister Trevino," he interrupted, "but I am obliged to shoulder the history of my own country. I could show you here the whole coming and going of the Mandan nation, wiped out in eighteen thirty-seven by a smallpox epidemic. I could show you how the arrival of German and Scandinavian farmers changed the composition of the topsoil, and the places where Charles Bodmer painted, and the evolution of red-light districts in Fargo—all that with pleasure. I've nothing against human passion, human longing. What I oppose is blind devotion to progress, and the venality of material wealth. If we're going to trade the priceless for the common, I want to know exactly what the terms are."

I had no response. His position was as difficult to assail as it would be to promote.

"You mean," I finally ventured, "that someone else will have to do the maps that show the spread of the Wal-Mart empire in North Dakota."

"I won't be doing those."

His tone was assertive but not testy. He wasn't even seeking my agreement.

"My daughter," I said, changing the subject, "wants to be an environmental historian. She has a good head for it, and I know she's interested—she wants to discover the kind of information you need to have to build a stable society. I'm sure it comes partly from looking at what's already there, as you suggest, like the birds this morning, how that movement, those movements, might determine the architecture of a society. I'm wondering—could I ever send her out? Maybe to help? Would you spend a few days with her?"

"I'd be glad to speak with her," he said, after considering the question. "I'd train her, if it came to that."

"Thank you."

He began squaring the maps up to place them back in the drawer.

"You know, Mister Trevino—Philip, if I may, and you may call me Corlis—the question is about you, really." He shut the drawer and gestured me toward the door of the room, which he closed behind us.

"You represent a questing but lost generation of people. I think you know what I mean. You made it clear this morning, talking nostalgically about my books, that you think an elegant order has disappeared, something that shows the way." We were standing at the corner of the dining table with our hands on the chair backs. "It's wonderful, of course, that you brought your daughter into our conversation tonight, and certainly we're both going to have to depend on her, on her thinking. But the real question, now, is what will *you* do? Because you can't expect her to take up something you wish for yourself, a way of seeing the world. You send her here, if it turns out to be what she wants, but don't make the mistake of thinking you, or I or anyone, knows how the world is meant to work. The world is a miracle, unfolding in the pitch dark. We're lighting candles. Those maps—they are my candles. And I can't extinguish them for anyone."

He crossed to his shelves and took down his copy of *The City of Geraniums*. He handed it to me and we went to the door.

"If you want to come back in the morning for breakfast, please do. Or, there is a cafe, the Dogwood, next to the motel. It's good. However you wish."

We said good night and I moved out through pools of dark beneath the ash trees to where I'd parked the car. I set the book on the seat opposite and started the engine. The headlights swept the front of the house as I turned past it, catching the salute of his hand, and then he was gone.

I inverted the image of the map from his letter in my mind and began driving south to the highway. After a few moments I turned off the headlights and rolled down the window. I listened to the tires crushing gravel in the roadbed. The sound of it helped me hold the road, together with instinct and the memory of earlier having driven it. I felt the volume of space beneath the clear, star-ridden sky, and moved over the dark prairie like a barn-bound horse.

VINTAGE BOOKS BY BARRY LOPEZ

About This Life

In *About This Life,* Barry Lopez turns, for the first time, to autobiographical reflections. Whether traveling to Antarctica or Bonaire, Hokkaido or the Galápagos, or remembering the California and New York of his childhood, Lopez probes the mysterious connections among landscape, memory, and imagination.

Literature/Nature/0-679-75447-4

Arctic Dreams

A National Book Award winner for nonfiction, *Arctic Dreams* is an unforgettable study of the Far North, the hauntingly pure land of stunted forests and frozen seas, of muskox and narwhal. Barry Lopez offers a stunning compendium of biology, anthropology, and history in this jubilant examination of the Arctic terrain and wildlife.

Natural History/0-375-72748-5

Crossing Open Ground

Barry Lopez weaves an invigorating spell in *Crossing Open Ground*. Through his crystalline vision, Lopez urges us toward a new attitude, a re-enchantment with the world that is vital to our sense of place, our well-being, and our very survival.

Literature/Nature/0-679-72183-5

Light Action in the Caribbean

This masterful collection of stories balances the marvelous and the real, the intellect and the heart, with extraordinary grace. Intelligent, precise, surprising, and unforgettable, these tales resonate with a knowledge of the world that transcends cultural and geographical borders, and they further secure Barry Lopez's reputation as one of our preeminent literary voices.

Fiction/Short Stories/0-679-75448-2

The Rediscovery of North America

Five hundred years ago, Christopher Columbus came to America and began a process not of discovery but of incursion—a "ruthless, angry search for wealth"—that continues today. This provocative book draws a direct line between the atrocities of the Spanish conquistadors and the ongoing pillage of our lands and waters, and challenges us to adopt an ethic that will make further depredations impossible.

Natural History/0-679-74099-6

Winter Count

In these resonant and unpredictable stories Barry Lopez uses a few deft strokes to produce painfully beautiful scenes: a flock of great blue herons descends through a snowstorm to the streets of New York; a ghostly herd of buffalo sings a song of death. Combining the real with the wondrous, he presents a vision of people alive to the immediacy and spiritual truth of nature.

Fiction/Short Stories/0-679-78141-2

VINTAGE **READERS**

Authors available in this series

Martin Amis

James Baldwin

Sandra Cisneros

Joan Didion

Richard Ford

Langston Hughes

Barry Lopez

Alice Munro

Haruki Murakami

Vladimir Nabokov

V. S. Naipaul

Oliver Sacks

Representing a wide spectrum of some of our most significant modern authors, the Vintage Readers offer an attractive, accessible selection of writing that matters.